M.

Steering 23 Publications
Milwaukee*Chicago

POETRY IN 13

Volume Three

a poetic Twitter Writing Community experience
edited by

SCOTT CHRISTOPHER BEEBE

Twitter Writing Community

anthologies edited by

Scott Christopher Beebe

Crispy Rooftop Conversation Stories

Hashtag The Horizon

Poetry in 13 **Volume One**

Prompting The Moon

Poetry in 13 **Volume Two**

Flashing Conversation Stories

Poetry in 13 **Volume Three**

released by *Steering 23 Publications*

All the poetry included in this anthology are original works by the author, each of whom are identified through their handles on Twitter. Their words are copyright protected by an assigned ISBN. Any reproduction of them must be granted in writing from the author(s).

TITLE Poetry In 13, Volume Three
EDITOR Scott Christopher Beebe
PUBLISHER Steering 23 Publications
DISTRIBUTOR KDP Select/Amazon.com company

COVER PHOTO Scott Christopher Beebe
TALENT COORDINATOR, LAYOUT/DESIGN
    Scott Christopher Beebe

FIRST PRINTING December, 2020

©2020

All rights reserved

Poetry In

13

Volume Three

Introduction

Twitter's Writing Community is vast, and consists of an outstanding group of people. For however worthy one would deem the value of a lifelong avid reader since taking their first step, I believe that many of its members arrange words in far superior ways than authors with high literary clout like Proust, Hemingway, King, Woolf, etc.

This is why I consider it such a high honor to have published many of their words to coincide with mine in our seventh anthology together.

To whom I would give even higher esteem would be the hundred-plus participants of #Poetryin13, a hashtag exercise for poets I created on Twitter in April, 2020 where I give them a daily word to weave 13-word poems around (and including) each prompt. The responses have been astounding.

What follows are some of these impressive efforts.

Scott Christopher Beebe
December 6, 2020
Milwaukee, WI

Note: **Prompt** words I gave are **highlighted.**

Dedication

This volume of poetry is dedicated to each and every person who took time out of their days which consist of otherwise busy schedules, least of which is a deadly worldwide pandemic (the novel coronavirus) to write such glorious words that made me laugh and cry; sometimes, both at once while experiencing a zenith of emotions.

I would also like to thank Mark, Voima, Arthur, Irene, Kelvin, Levi, DeRicki, Alva, Steve and the rest of the Flash Dogs for bringing #vss365 to Twitter. It will always be home to me.

And last but not least, to my M.

'Cause I never...

Table Of Contents

@andylectablyme 21
@OminousHallways 24
@CatwomanJS 27
@Ms_Took 31
@chandanas 33
@sanjaraic1 36
@genevatow 39
@Kat_Kacker 42
@SmartyMarty1126 45
@EHHarperPoetry 48
@AliceCurleyPoetry 51
@MontyVern 53
@CatherineBeavis 56
@Musiker_123 59
@AdamJanBarry 62
@LizKyfer 65
@NoNeed2BStrong 68
@MescalTess 70
@MommyMyaw 72
@Raijori 75
@Goddess_ov_soul 78
@MattKWrites 80
@EarthschoolH 83
@JessicaLaymon5 85
@TriciaSanky 88
@SentientOnes 91

@ThomasHartigan   94
@MatzMusings   95
@OMANXL1   99
@TheSurrealAri   100
@JEM1979   103
@Barbara52744094   106
@MyNameIsAshleeC   109
@ArvindSoliloquy   112
@MelissaG1954   115
@GaleMeadows801   118
@PlayPlaceNovel   121
@Free2BMac   123
@HotmaiBill   125
@MadQueenStorm   128
@Pixie0_0   131
@Upasika1   134
@JuneNightOwl   137
@BrianJohn2Jule1   138
@FrankieInParis   141
@JBeanHibbs   144
@CJ_Firelights   147
@tblend3   150
@WingedWriter90   153
@NadXim   154
@ThatLousyNick   157
@fuller_edward   160
@DXMarieAuthor   162
@CallMeChel_324   165

@HyKuWriter 167
@AlanVMichaels 170
@joypainlovewrit 173
@CoCoEssences 176
@Scribbled_Lines 179
@DrGeetaBhandari 182
@JoyEnzed 185
@MarshaWritesIt 188
@KEMWriting 191
@IriePoetry 194
@TsukoakariUsagi 197
@WhiskeySourHour 200
@moomooseum 203
@fhaedra 206
@AnnaBurnsWrites 209
@Mark_Nificent 212
@Patrici30730227 215
@faxtors 218
@hills1s 221
@theedemaruh 224
@serene_she 227
@somaxdatta 230
@EdHaiku575 232
@TalwaiSarita 235
@ncscrolls 238
@MelJ_Writes 241
@Mila255h 243
@MariaAPerez1 245

@TheLadyMagic   248
@LeahBoudreaux2   250
@KrypticKro   253
@WDFBarry   256
@ByThisWillAlone   259
@Loverno87785276   262
@HayleyReeseChow   264
@WeitWrite   267
@LRHudgins   270
@Pallavi31   272
@DMDavanti   275
@heath_laws   278
@JPGarlandAuthor   281
@MoSchoenfeld   284
@IpsaHerself   287
@WhatsUpNowHun   290
@SarikaJaswani   292
@ColinBevis11   295
@David_McTigue   298
@megwaf   301
@shifting_void   304
@ImPaul23   307
@cross_hali   310
@EJ_Reine   313

@ProsSpeaks   316
@Stull_Mitchell   319
@ChamomileSpells   322
@WittyNameSoon   325
@Jap3DUpHeart   326
@rajivindia   329
@sonaprojai08   332
@wvineet1   333
@aflametarot   336
@ideanumvber13   339
@smitchelwrites   341
@free_thinkerist   343
@JeanRoeMartin   346
@vlad_lioncourt   349
@yonar   350
@SpiritdDrmWeavr   353
@Ponderoda   354
@DaniGraceWrites   355
@FizzyTwizler   358
@starfish_72   361
@juliusorolovsky   364
@storysmithscb   367

Epilogue

FEAR   371

ⒶANDYLECTABLYME

While we thought
We were
Solving
Life's mystery
Life
Was secretly
Unravelling
Us

        *

I'd willingly be
A **hostage**
Of your love
Yet
You set me
Free

        *

To articulate emotions
He **scattered** them
On paper
Hoping for words
To speak

*

To be lost
In the **woods**
Of your memories
Never to be found

*

You cannot **summon**
Peace
To your mind
If you enjoy
The chaos around

*

When life **shreds** you
To the basest of your emotions
Let Hope triumph.

*

It is an inconvenience
When words
Interfere
With emotions
Being shared
In silence

*

Genesis of unhappiness
Is more to do with
Unjustifiable needs
Than unfulfilled wants

*

Be wary
Of the thoughts
That you **entertain**.
Some guests
Tend to overstay

@OminousHallways

Due to circumstances
Beyond our control
All current circumstances
Are beyond our control

*

Box of chocolates
I'll just have
A **couple**
Then some
More
More
All

*

You **stabbed** my heart
But you said I'm heartless

The joke's on you!

*

He went from
Here to
Paternity

Instantly
His life
Filled with

Pure love

    *

Politics creates **battlegrounds**

Inventing false enemies

False narratives

People suffer

Just wanting peace

    *

Encased in cavernous darkness
Will I emerge in light?
Or will mysteries **deepen**?

*

The **discrepancy**
Between
How I see
The world
And how it
Sees me

*

Smoke
From the
Fire
Of our love
Obfuscates
And **suffocates**
My dying
Heart

*

Heartstrings cut
Mourning dove **topples**
Into the dead leaves
Where my love decays

(4)CATWOMANJS

The words
Went **away**
It feels
As if
My heart
Went with them

*

Constantly
Needing
To be in
The **limelight**
Turned her
Deep green
With envy

*

Is there
Anywhere
We can feel safe
Anymore
That's not full of
Loneliness

                    *

The **Virga** symbolized
There was a place
It didn't rain
On my parade

                    *

All that **glitters**
Is not gold or stars
Sometimes it's just
Fish scales

                    *

Don't jump
On the **bandwagon**
Roll with the wheels
In your own head

*

I **summon**
That held
Deep within
And put
My pen
To paper
Poetry

*

Syzygy confuses me
In solar system symmetry
And same sounding letters
In Poetry

*

Just **being**
For now
Warmth on hold
Hope I'll thaw
When it's over

@Ms_Took

You **ransacked** my breathing under the Pine trees...
Then, I slowly asphyxiated yours.

*

I am nothing.
Just an idea.

Until,

Fragments of
nebulas and intentions collaborated.

*

Underneath **countless** stars, my soul often dreamt.
And then, solace embraces my mind.

*

Swept me away beneath
the oneiric tide pools...
And serenade me with stardust.

*

Particles
of your shadow
sing to me-

A willing captive
of your memory.

*

Books have **vertebraes** and wings...

But not all men have spines and imaginations.

*

My sun rises
in the turquoise
lagoon...

But, my mind
is a barmecide.

*

I **retrieved** the
swirls of
borrowed memory...

And fade into
somewhere in
between.

*

Wish I can forget
that nudiustertian
sunset...
Of **rapturous** caresses
and of betrayal

*

Lies **froth**
in the lips
of those
who drank
from the
same cup

(4) CHANDANAS

It's magical
when dreams waltz,
butterflies **flutter**,
flowers smile,
even when
autumn features…

*

Away,
  far away
    from formality of love,
let's unite in ceremony of love!

*

Fragments of time
patch memories together,
into fabric of life,
stitch by stitch.

*

I make
countless trips
to your barren eyes,
to find love in them.

*

Held **hostage** to each others' memories,
we seek ransom to relive our togetherness.

*

In **market**,
a heart in despair,
craves repair,
attracts bidders,
but no healers.

*

with phases of moon,
with changes in season,
we blossomed;

efflorescence of love!

*

a **plethora** of emotions,
she's deific, she's fire
she creates,
she can destroy.

*

On **nook** of
his shoulder,
the sun sets,
in her eyes,
it rises.

*

Basking in
the **afterglow**
of love,
a smile
caught a
coy lambent hue.

@SANJARAIC1

Shivers ran
down his spine
when
she **exposed** herself
within the golden hour.

*

She writes slowly
unravelling words
bringing together
fragments of laughter &
bursts of fear.

*

Morning **murmuring**
Its first words
Mists caressing
Hillsides
Tenderness of
An imaginary kiss.

*

An aborted gesture
a **suspended** gaze
a breath held
in expanse of twilight.

*

December,
portent of love
or **imposter**
not knowing
where to
make me go...

*

She **galvanizes** him
with her
Eden of words
whispered in
an incessant
Back-and-forth.

*

The comet's tail
punches leaden
November sky
filling my heart
with precipitous
serenity.

*

A sudden gust
of peculiar loneliness
scattered the
light of
the waxing Moon.

*

Moss on pines
Inhaling
November mist
As his pen
Ransacks snow
Humming
Warmblood.

(4) GeneVatow

My fingers race
up and down the **frets**
Jam turned into a riff

*

Her love came from **afar**
to rescue me
and hold me forever dear

*

The length
and breadth
of life
is a collaboration
formed whole
from **fragments**

*

Together
we render
quondam shadows
into the amazing
and brilliant
reality of today

*

Key by key
he stretched
these zealous images
of trees
in the **woods**

*

How lonely
is the heart of bravery
Bombarded by
the truth of love

*

Compendium of solace
Blanketed across the world
like the **countless** stars
at night

*

Magic
weaving freedom
Oneiric in the night
boundaries overflowing
swept toward the light

*

Whispers find investment
in the wasteland
of a soul..

Seafarers know it best.

*

Thumbing through pages
of a year gone **askew**
tinged with sadness
painted blue…

@Kat_Hacker

Pieces **scatter**
consumed by absolute darkness
fading into nothingness.

Trying to hold on.

*

Instincts **immerse** me
in truths I can
no longer deny.
I face myself.

*

Embers fading,
summer's final bonfire
succumbs to winter's chill
as I **diminish** too.

*

Being too present
in my past
burns long-scarred
layers into
open wounds.

*

Murmuring fills the expanse
where her footprints stopped.
Pale streetlight the silent witness.

*

Feverish pacing
contract tracing
trying to capture
semblance of calm.
This mad world.

*

Unseen **visitor**
aerialist descends from sky
blowing dreams across continents,
consoling grieving hearts.

*

We **summon**
hints of bravery
with empty hands
as wobbly uncertainty
threatens sanity.

*

We hate to admit,
being **penniless**
brings with it
deep humiliation and shame.

*

Driving home through **fog**
alone.
Tears fall in the silence of
your absence.

*

I run through
every hospital **corridor**
searching,
screaming inside,
afraid you're already gone.

@SMARTYMARTY1126

Immaculate in
her beauty
She gallops
across the plains
Chased by the sun

*

Becoming a writer
Takes more than mere
Paper and #ink
Much courage
is necessary

*

His forked tongue
reveals his identity
Nevertheless
his followers hold him
in reverence

*

What a feat it
will be!
We shall **retrieve**
the courage
of kindness.

*

Savage time
ravages the heart
But it can not
diminish
our love affair

*

Beyond the **windowpane**
lies a world of promise
Inside, a captive of fear

*

With each signature
we assured
our nation isn't
a joke **anymore**
Democracy reborn

*

All of us, **robust**
in body and spirit
Our hearts, excited
with possibilities

*

My **restless** soul
doomed to forever
scare the living
Actually, they
frighten me

From **across** the room
I hear your heart
Beating in sync with mine

@EHarperPoetry

These **fragments**—shards
of you, once my favorite
pain, now just blood
stains.

*

Scatter me like a puzzle,
examine each piece
and make me whole again

*

My soul
is the ultimate

imposter,

lying about trying

as I lay dying.

*

A ghost
I long to be

afar from reality

haunting your dreams
eternally.

*

Cut
my soul
into pieces,
pack me in **boxes**,
and set me free.

*

Punch me
leave bruises
of black and blue
a galaxy to remember you.

*

You looked past my pain,
ransacked my being
and stole my whole soul.

*

The pain
was long
and death
was quick.
Dead, not
alive, not
anymore.

*

Your luminous eyes
looked inside of me

Now my agony
is finally **pacified**.

@AliceCurleyPoet

Dreams are **visitors** with answers
We forget by morning
Unless a premonition insists

*

Standing beside you
Playing it cool
My heart **murmuring**
With memories of us

*

I discovered my pent up feelings **unraveling** as your long overdue apology unfolded.

*

You walked **away** casually
Knowing my heart would be
Shattered by your departure

*

Her eyes **glistened**
With pent up tears
As she let go of him

*

Absorb the relief
You are still afraid to feel
It is real

(4) Monty Vern

Secrets **exposed** down to raw flesh and bones; I emerge ugly and free.

*

Sometimes the kindest thing I can do is to stay **away** from you.

*

He **murmurs** to my inner ear that I'm not worthy of anyone's tears.

*

Suspended with the finest filaments; I dance obediently to the master puppeteer's whimsy.

*

Honesty turned out to be an **imposter**; Integrity exposed my lies and disingenuity.

*

Haggled me up; **haggled** me down; turned my pockets inside-out and upside down.

*

Face reddened;
Bursting and angered;
Chess pieces **scattered**;
Check-mate thwarted;
Another beating awarded.

*

I couldn't carry the weight **anymore**; I faltered and fell; life moved along.

*

Rustic and **robust**;
Spiced to entice;
Seductively savory;
Her red sauce delights me.

*

Knot me with your **entanglements** and I'll come loose to trip you up.

*

Propel me please from this meeting of the dull minds and incurious souls.

*

Her first love story blackened with twists and turns in the **campfire** flames.

*

Rising from depths of depression; glimpses of perspective; renewal; a new **apotheosis** coming.

(4)CatherineBeavis

My dear
l Dream
Of us together,

Longing
For you,
But
From
Afar

*

My heart
Will always
sing
And soar
With **particles**
Of our
Unforgettable
Love

*

Wishing
I could
immerse
Myself
In
Your
Arms
To heal
My
Broken soul

*

Reindeer
Never
Fret
Soaring over
Silent
Skies
Invisible wings
Helps flying
All night

*

I **summon**
The clouds
To rain
On me
Concealing
Tears of
Perpetual
Pain

*

My love
I'll **bombard**
You with
Fudge
And we'll
Share the
Sweetness
Together

*

The comforting **campfire**
Dries my tears
If only it could
Vanquish
My fears

ⓐMUSIKER_123

Unravelling memories,
Haunting me with each appearance,
How much more can I take?

*

Don't **fret** or you'll regret,
The memories you knew best,
Oh yes.

*

I shall **summon**,
All of my courage,
Just to continue,
Just to heal.

*

Every part of my **being** aches for even more of you to love.

*

I am **becoming** myself,
I am finally doing well,
Sadness, go to hell!

*

You swept me into your arms,
Away from all of the world's harm.

*

I held you in my arms,
You held me **hostage**,

I'll hold myself.

*

My heart is stuck in an eternal **loop**,
it chases after only you.

ⒶADAMIANBARRY

Embers glowing.
In a humble.
Pan of ash.
With effortless.
Sparkling.
Warming.
Panache.

*

Raindrops.
Teardrops.
Synchronistically soothing.
Swept.
Wept.
Flushing out pain.
Healing flowing to brain.

*

An **Apotheosis**.
A Prognosis of Success.
An Osmosis of Synthesis.
A Seismic Theology.

*

Being penniless.
Entrust nobody **anymore.**
Sequester
Rambunctious
Feelings
In deep **woods.**
Fearing success.

*

Getting jobs done.
Creating more than consuming.
Get to rest more.
Not **restless.**

*

My protons connected.
Excitedly.
With your protons.
And celebrated.
An energized.
Particles party.

*

Wings.
Unconsciously.
Clipped.
Caged.
Journeying.
Inwards.
Quantum.
Seagull.
Cavalry.
Jailbird.
Flying.
Free.

*

So much to do.
Sewing strands.
Together we can.
Galvanize.
Each other's.
DNA.

@LIZKYFER

Gazing deep into
Patterns of frost
Hoping to **expose**
traces
of my path.

*

Trying to remember
Love's amputated touch
Severed too long ago
Too far **away**.

*

Words **murmuring**
on the screen
Undo me
More than
any
remembered
touch
Has.

*

Unseen, you **glisten**
in my treasured thought
No less cherished
for being impossible.

*

She learned
Not to be deaf,
so **absorbed**
in thought.
She misses it.

*

Boxed
Struggling to climb out
Until I look
and see
your outstretched hand.

*

Becoming something new?
Or just pulling illusion
Over my head to sleep again?

*

Your words from **afar**.
Can't touch or hold them but
they hold me.

*

Carefully fitting
fragments into place
When gluing is done
Mirror shows new face.

*

Left door ajar
you would be
a most welcome **visitor**
in my dreams.

(A)NONEED2BSTRONG

what use bread **Afar**
when Mother downs gin
and Father shoots up sugar?

*

Suspend
the work of cash
indefinitely
and hire
the fire of love.
Now.

(4)MescalTess

fog drifts through my mind
stabbing doubt follows
what lies in wait there?

*

the susurrus of **murmurings**
from my mouth to your ear
listen closely now

*

flowers and
glistening leaves
perfume wafting
eyes among the foliage
awake and watching

*

along with **entanglements**
caring must follow
else self-serving
is all we are…

                *

disasters **propel** us forward
calm sailing tends to take us
in lazy circles

                *

across the heavens
between deep oceans and tall trees
within whispering distance
stardust…

                *

for my Melbourne…

running **interference**
cannot allow distraction
one role
one mission
eyes on the prize…

*

seasonal **repercussions** advance
too much heat and wind
too soon
conflagration imminent
m'aidez…

*

countless stars gaze
down each night
blessing us
with light and
twinkle, twinkle…

*

knowing where
the **trapdoor** is
does not explain
why it waits for you...

ⒶMommyMyaw

what would it take
to **galvanize** people
to take action against
a tyrant?

*

there is no **haggling** allowed
in my shop;
just take what you want

*

break my heart
scatter the pieces
I fall apart
and the world ceases

*

How to leave a room
without being awkward?
You do it with **panache**!

*

walking home **penniless**
pondering my loneliness
fighting against hunger
afraid of helpful strangers

*

groping blindly
in the dark
the **trapdoor**
closed above
her screams
go unheard

*

bombard my heart
with love instead of lies
and I will be yours

*

I keep you with me always
in tiny little **boxes** where you belong

*

ransack my mind
hijack my soul
take my body hostage
don't let go

*

here I am
reminiscing
a **quondam** love
in the midst of the rain

*

they told me
to be **cautious**
for love is deep
i still fell

*

I don't want to be sappy
but I've been a fan from **afar**

(4)Raijori

Trapdoor with
Skin **texture**.
Countless wails
Entangled behind.
Come **along**,
Bask in screams.

*

[Memory **Showcase**]
Norman **Bates** --
Jailbird...
Lovebird...
Swept under bed.
First **becoming**,
First kill.

*

Seafarer --
Hostage of digital
Stream.
Askew immersion
Among godless
Particles.
Stripped naked...
Childless.

*

Foggy mind
Restless twitch,
Drifting through
Second hand
Organ **market.**
Propelled stab...
Release.

*

Silent **campfire**
Diminished across
The Time
Not reaching advocates
Of **Eternal Lofty** Flame

*

You!
Just a **husk**.
Proved your **deft**,
Reaching
Immaculate Apotheosis
Not **enmeshed**.
Welcome!

*

Shadows **circulate**
Empty **corridors**
Shredding souls
Inbetween.
Without **repercussions**.
Without Angels
To **interfere**.

*

Tumultuous sneeze
Catapulted windowpane.
Aerodynamic squeeze
Completely insane.
'Tis **efflorescence**
In present tense.

@GODDESS_OV_SOUL

Fog lifted
first clear sight
my eyes & your eyes
Gaze Locked tight

*

she is a spawn of stars
a starchild
drowning in midnight
Sparkling magic

*

Within the **interlude** of rain & sunlight streaming
a rainbow happened
Prettyfully

*

countless threads weaved & tangled into us
enmeshed from the other side

*

Breath upon my neck
my heartbeats pause
Breathless
Breathe again
Your **interference**
magical

*

expose my bones
of these butterflies
RAWR'ing deep inside
setting free
flying wild

*

entrust love within yourself
your heart is a bank
GROWING your LOVE deposit

@MattKWrites

Around the **campfire**
They scare and fright
With marshmallows
and death
all night

              *

So much **panache**
The despair never registered
When the diagnosis
of death came

              *

Look through the **boxes**
My common sense
and sanity
Have to be somewhere

              *

Where is your meat
I was told
his **market**
has the freshest
human

*

Tear away the **husk**
and a corn cob
will scream
a horrible screech

*

I **entrust**
these words
to you
Use them wisely
Or toss them away

*

The Phoenix
His **quondam** friend
Now a meal
It would not
rise again

*

Put it in print
Might **entertain**
Could fall flat
Don't
And never know

*

The world put through
the **shredder**
Taping it back together
will take time

*

The **countless** times
you have cried
Still you find solace
In a lie

ⓐEARTHSCHOOLH

Do you see it?
Light moves
And **glistens**
Reminding us
Life's a dance

*

Shimmering
lake ripples
reach out
touching shore
perpetual motion
all things are
Connected

*

In a world
Seemingly **fractured**
Breathe
Love and kindness
Like healing balm
Awaits

*

Visitors
This moment in time
Just passing through
Eternity
All else
Falls away

*

The awakening
Unravels slowly
Whispers
From beyond the veil
Resonate
Puzzle pieces
Gifted

*

I journeyed
Into the white
Now back
I'm **suspended**
Somewhere between
two worlds

@JESSICALAYMON5

There was no recourse except to **punch** it, run; she didn't get far.

*

He **summoned** and rejected his demons.
She has always embraced and loved hers.

*

From the closet,
Murmuring
Of two voices.
Turned the handle
To find nothing.

*

He left behind his **husk** and released the rest to roam the earth.

*

Its gaunt face looked at me
And I knew it wasn't alive, **anymore.**

*

And then it happened,
His soul **suspended**
From the ground.
A faceless spectacle.

*

I am **scattered** me
Sent to chase after wild dreams
Of wilder seas.

*

Overwhelmed
By
The
World
Right
Now.

Call back later.
Or, not at all.

(A)TRICIA SANKEY

Sequester my heart with yours,
cocoon with silk,
and I'll never fly away.

*

Can't wax poetic
you **scatter** my thoughts
Read my mind
with this kiss

*

You left me
     an inept **seafarer**
        alone
in a boat
    full
       of
          holes.

*

Cupid
Punched my
Heart black

But at least
he got it
Beating
Again

     *

He stared so long
her face flushed
and the world
    just
      drifted
        away.

     *

Don't **fret** as I dive,
     in silent twists -

the spinning sun is soft.

     *

He **shredded** flowers and sprinkled them loosely over the grave he just dug.

*

I was broken in **countless** ways. Until your hands sewed a beautiful patchwork.

*

I'm a **jailbird**
in treehouse,
tweeting
into clouds
with mouths
like a cat.

*

Galvanized memories
of me and you
my hearts dark corner
your endless tomb

*

(4)SentientOnes

Fragments of me
shall be found in you
whenever you search for yourself.

*

The **restless** churning inside me
needs the zephyr of your presence
that soothes.

*

Unravelling the
secrets of the heart
is an art, you are adept at.

*

Sequestered
I became a poem
and the poet
the peace and the riot.

*

wish to write happy
but breeze rushes in through the **windowpane**
spreading disdain.

*

the sapid breeze
enmeshed with your memories
it catches and holds
my soul.

*

The rise to the moon
propels dreams
and sometimes moon dust falls down.

*

We **collaborated** to pick up fragments
of each other to walk some steps together.

*

She pours dew
over the hinges of the stuck up **trapdoor**
of memories.

*

The cleft
speaks in **deft** tones
silencing the din around
without a sound.

*

He loves me more
        when I **interfere**

I make sure
        chance is there.

*

A **tumultuous** year
brought new challenges
and fears
a quiet smile
and tear.

@THOMASHARTIGAN

She **ransacks** my heart
Her eyes melt into my soul
Enveloped loving

*

Manifest [your]
Destiny
No more
Rest you see
Just the best of me

*

Will humanity
Disembark from Earthship
With COVID-19 as our
Passport to the afterlife?

*

The invisible
Are divisible
Be visible
When seen the visible
Are always **indivisible**

@MATZMUSINGS

The Moon
chooses
Not to judge Us,
as We **scatter**
toward Her
shadows.

*

For I have
no Muse
to **summon**,
pages
before me
remain,
forever
blank.

*

We are but final glowing embers
of an autumn **campfire**
soon to extinguish.

*

Love
ripped apart,
like pages
from a novel.
Fragments
scattered
into the Winds.

*

Bound,
to hollow
memories,
Chained,
to a **sequestered**
Heart,
Forever,
a Lovelorn
Slave.

*

In this
unfortunate
instance,
being pierced
by Cupid's Arrow,
proved to be

*

Stars navigated
from a
quondam night,
guided
My wending,
leading me,
to You.

*

Rumbling Clouds,
began **murmuring**,
as wicked Winds,
started their howl.
The Mountains,
shivered.

*

Boxes of stars,
kept under her bed,
released
on nights,
when feeling
homesick

ⓐOMANXL1

She was intergalactic / universal but also self destructive; she **ransacked** the galaxy within

*

Place your hands up **imposter**! Misplaced key in the land of dust and emptiness?

*

From **afar**? It seemed secure / locked inside but I found the misplaced key

*

Pardon me for being **rambunctious**..

Bound by words! The gathering? I'll interrupt this

*

I was warned; the higher power would **entrust** me with a complex magic..

*

Attacked! I had to **summon** the Supreme Courage that resides deep down inside

*

You have to zoom in to Follow The Light! It's far far **away**

*

I'll embark on a celestial journey..

Just trying to **salvage** the infernal wreckage

@THESURREALARI

Find yourself reflected in the **windowpane**—

Your debut in the world of spirits.

*

Light shines in multifarious refractions
Through the cold **froth** of my pint glass

*

A flower
Its petals **shred** by life
Still yearns upward
Toward the sun

*

The king of the alley
Holds court on his throne
An overturned **box**

*

The mysteries of the universe
Refracted in the infinite permutations
Of creation's **afterglow**

*

In the silence of the void
The universe prevaricates
Between **being** and unbeing

*

You see a couple of beautiful roses **intertwined**

but not the thorns underneath.

*

The butterfly **flutters** around the anachronistic aerial
Beating back signals from the past.

*

After so many years
The dead phoenix reborn
Doesn't surprise me
Much **anymore**

*

Quarantine
Everyone's home
And I'm sitting here
Nostalgic for those silent,
Solitary
Interludes.

*

Time out of mind
Mind out of time
Forever trapped
In this **loop**

*

The **obstreperous** youth
May be stronger than me

But I will sift through

@JEM1979

Our bodies
are merely **husks**,
and when they
perish,
our souls
continue on.

for Melbi
RIP

*

I held him close,
shaking and spent,
utterly vulnerable
in perfect, brilliant
afterglow.

*

I loved you
from **afar**,
always seen
but never noticed,
memory's lost
Reflection.

*

I long for
restless adventure,
flying on wings
of wood and steel
forever.

*

I've left my heart
in the **Highlands**,
lost among the
heather strewn
lanes.

*

Sickening feelings
right before the
bough breaks,
a **catapult**
waiting to jump-start
history.

*

Sprinkles
of gold
softly falling,
sunset
whispering that
soon everything
will be understood

*

You ascend
like ancient Pharaohs,
glorified light
illuminating all,
the **apotheosis**
of nature.

ⒶBARBARA52744094

translational
seasons
woods cloaked
in leaves of
red and gold
natures
untamed forest

*

loves thirst
pacified
by winter's night
perfect rhythm
cradled
in alter
of desires

*

trapdoor
of silence
lays still on
winter's blanket
snowflakes pour
In morning
solitude

*

gentle breezes
murmuring
in velvet shadows
of winters
affairs
whispers of hearts
despair

*

free
and **cautious**
november leaves
fall
becoming part
of nature's landscape
autumn's release

*

restless dreams
frozen in
amethyst night
voices scream
insomnia bleeding
demons
claim silence

*

yesterday's dreams
immersed
through mirror's soul
looking backwards
images
disguised as
october's serenade

*

autumns
southern sunset
advocate of silence
like loves verses
waiting to be
finished

@MyNameIsAshleeC

you don't need
a guiding light
anymore

you've become
your own
beautiful beacon

*

I reused **fragments**
of words
that were trimmed
from other poems
to explain

*

the warmth of you
beside me
studying the sky
next to a **campfire**

*

we can **bombard**
this world with healing
without alienating anyone
-my hope forward

⁎

a **shred** of simplicity
amongst the chaotic world
a flower to a bee

⁎

love notes,
written on hotel stationary
for me to find,
propel anticipation-

tonight…

⁎

your caring eyes
relieved the **stabbing** pain
in my heart
and distracted me

⁎

there will be days
that **glisten**
in their memory
visited over and over

          *

fingertips
swept across
my shoulder blades

only the wind
was behind me

breathe

          *

a dense **entanglement**
of vines
on a steep embankment
harbor
glory for morning

(4) ARVIND SOLILOQUY

Silent Pond
Stray Ripples
Breeze rolls in Dried leaves
Murmuring to rumbling ensues

*

Sky Blue
Sunlit Hue
Hurried Dew

A Hungry Mew
Imposter Weather
Camouflaging Untrue

*

Dark Night
Clouds choking Starlight
Hope withering

Shadows **summon** fear
Keeping panic intact

*

Wistful gaze
Lingering wish
Stray **visitor**

Sprinkling holy water
Over my numb existence

*

Each morning brings
Hope
Like dew
Scattered on leaves
Scintillating
In a Hurry

*

Bows caressing
The rough skinned trunks
Feverish self Love
Lights up blue forest

*

Why **pacify**
Rectify
Redress

Done knowingly
To hurt
Injure
Impair
Damage

To Polarise

ⒶMELISSAG1954

Snow **glistened**
on her lashes
as she prayed
for a Christmas
miracle

*

Can you hear me
murmuring
Thoughts of love
and happiness,
for us all?

*

Play me like a guitar
til I beg
for fingers on the **frets**

*

Too afraid
to go too far
She makes
a wish
on stars
afar

*

My **scattered** thoughts
wax poetic
while I dream of
your wicked, tasty smiles

*

Ransacking your way through
my thoughts
you leave a stained trail
of betrayal

*

Don't live your life based on **quondam**
Look ahead and live with zest

*

Entertain me
with your twilight kiss
Savage, groping emotions
leaving us forever entwined

*

Countless memories
Endless nights
Never stop
Holding me tight
Our love
Is forever

*

You **propel** my
heart into light
all while setting
fire to my nights

*

How will she survive
the **tumultuous** goodbye
with shorter days
and longer nights?

@GALEMEADOWS801

Whirlwind of emotion
My love for you growing
Each day I fall faster

*

Caught in the wreckage
I'll **salvage** pieces
Of my broken heart
Reconstruct myself

*

Absorb my sorrow
Wrap me in your arms
Hold me together
Encompassing love

*

Feverish desire
My want of you returns
Make my fantasies real
Satisfy hunger

*

Nothing can **pacify**
My thirst for him
The hunger grows
Craving passion
Wanting

*

Envisioning you
Thoughts **unravelling**
Imagination thrills
Your words
Stirring emotions
I want you

*

Suspend my heart in silence
It always belonged to you
Lost in darkness

*

Loving you from **afar**
Like the horizon kisses the sky
Yet never meets

*

Hide myself in you
Galvanize two hearts together
Lost souls now at home

*

I'm held **hostage** to emotion
Lost in your darkness
All consuming silence screams

*

I **immerse** myself inside of your darkness
Forgetting who I am
Without you

@PlayPlaceNovel

Your calves by
My neck **effervesce**
The need to
Pull you in harder

*

Your legs are
Shaking in anticipation
Knowing they **mirror**
What they'll do later

*

Your words leave me in
A state of **acquiescence**,
Falling in love again

ⒶFREE2BMAC

Grinning,
        spinning
    from toes
        to her nose
dripping with sweat
  whirlwind she shows

          *

Did they just creep in
No wonder aliens rule
lofty stars night sky

          *

Spray me sparingly
sprinkle or mist,
from goddess lips
heaven sent a kiss

          *

missing her, you breathe
on the **windowpane**, spelling
her name in the moisture

*

emergency exits when
life slips us into a
ditch, kindness,
joy, hope, love

*

we go round
and **circulate**
hand in hand
hearts conjunct
converge our fate

*

What brought trust,
entanglements,
locked fingers,
locked arms,
locked legs,
together as one

*

Pockets **penniless**,
the laughter I
provide when you
look at me is gold

*

your love flows
from hearts
at shore
as the riptide
pulls you **afar**

*

Words unspoken
tension displayed
silence breaks
unraveling you stray
love revealed
time **away**

*

motionless to canvas
preserve our moment
but a few strokes
of the brush

@HOTMAIBILL

all is eden
nevertheless
a begging earth
does not touch
the wondrous sky

*

when the sun **glistens**
melts upon itself,
wishes soak the ground
fiery exhortations

*

reaching into the mist
the midst of **quondam** light
hazier, but warming still.

*

fading like a desert mirage
was her satiny presence
a mesmerizing optical illusion?

*

galvanize like steel
shine with invulnerability,
with a superhero boldness,
humankind speeds ahead.

*

never alone, thinking again,
speaking in strained silence,
an analytical **soliloquy**,
antithetical thoughts.

*

particles magnetize
while the mind
overanalyzes,
keeping in place
a blasted
taut equilibrium.

*

air lifts us,
we **propel**
over cloth clouds
penny pictures,
hearts anxiously soar.

*

surreptitious whispers
heard in doorways,
bending 'round corners,
clandestine sounds,
of one's living.

@MadQueenStorm

Don't **diminish** yourself to make anyone else feel better. Keep your shine strong.

*

becoming his willing prey
she surrenders
the spell of his lips
her undoing

*

silence can **shred** a soul
strip nerve from bone
waiting for words unwritten

*

give me the knife
I'll **stab** myself
in the heart
it'll be faster

*

The **genesis** of pain, a shattered heart and broken bond. Life becomes meaningless.

*

the maelstrom within
broken open
spilling **fragments**
like chaotic snow
drifting into cracks

*

an abandoned shell
made of scars
the remnant **husk**
of a dessicated heart

*

wandering **afar**
a long journey
into night
the ties that bind
coming undone

*

her's was a wind-**swept** heart
one of rolling storms
& thunderous loves

        *

Closing my eyes, I **immerse** myself in the voices of the sighing winds.

        *

held **hostage** by memories
a surplus of existential pain
replayed over and over

        *

a single **slice**
one for each wrist
the day I died
yet lived

        *

Being alone is nothing new to me, but it does get really lonely.

@PIXIE0_0

Tumultuous rainfall
sweeping wandering
parched leaves
upon the wickedness of
obstreperous autumn wind

*

kiss my words
turn them into poetry
catapulting
heart,
abnegation of my being

*

Happiness,
Lies inside of your heart
I realized it with
stab of time

*

Two stray clouds
collide
galvanize
into
soft rain

The wind played its part

*

Your **immaculate** light
blinded my sight
like a nomad
I follow you everywhere

*

...

nail some stars
in the **vertebrae** of night
dive
    I
      N
        T
          O
my waning moonlight

*

I circulate
around you
My only universe
the way moon
around the Sun

*

your
salty nature
erodes my beauty
sinked me in
theorem of
miscalculated
affection

*

collect my broken petals
coalesce into a rose
tie me in your braid

(4) UPASIKA1

I will guard
your memories
in my soul
Against
the **thievery**
of time

*

Hoping against hope,
Do keep on believing,
Never let life
interfere with living!

*

An unrepentant **jailbird**
this rebellious soul,
Serving the sentence
of life without parole!

*

Burdens fall away
when I see
the **genesis** of hope
in your eyes

*

I **preserve**
the faded tints
of old roses
lovingly
in reams of memory...

*

Always **cautious**,
tried to steer clear
of pitfalls,
Ironically unable
to avoid manholes!

*

Fields of ages **swept**
by winds of time,
Great hand destroys
and resurrects!

*

Pursuit of happiness -
A temporary relief
To **suspend** my disbelief,
Life is suffering.

*

Unapologetically me
Never compromised
to fit into
any of the
boxes of society

*

Those teardrops
that could not fall
from my eyes,
Listen to them **glisten**...

*

Shine your light
Flickering firefly
I am not
Out of the **woods** yet...

@JuneNightOwl

My heart
Asks not
To be **preserved**

My heart
Asks
To be loved

*

Muted morning light
Effused through blinds
And **afterglow**
Illuminating his face
His smile

*

Crossing her mind daily
He left
An indelible **zigzag** pattern
On her heart

@BRIANJOHNYULE1

Held out 'til she was so **feverish**
She couldn't taste the bitter pill

*

Drifting away
The predawn **sifting**
Haunts listless slumber
Unstill & humbled
Shattered road

*

Unravelling together
Our frayed edges tangled
Knots of nervous intimacy
Forming from collapse

*

The dawn sun
An unwelcome **visitor**
Shedding dreary light
On their fresh grief

*

Caught **uncautious**
Like Samson unlocked
Drunk on newfound vulnerability
This ecstasy of doubt

*

Robust numbers resist
With stubborn clarity
As tunnelvision experience suborns denial
Facts persist

*

Outside serenity
Countless sinners
Knock on the cell door
In search of solace

*

Immersed in meadowfoam nectar
Deputised to cross the threshold
Feaster feeds a future

*

Electromagnetic whispers
Amidst cosmic noise
Phoenix ashes of yesteraeons
Propelled beyond heatdeath's light

*

They found us
Enmeshed in each other
Mutually inflamed
Naked & unashamed
Aglow

*

Repercussions of your words' incision
My shell prized open
A shucked oyster
Awaiting

④FRANKIEINPARIS

She waited
For the **trapdoor**
To swallow the turtle
Stuck on his back

*

"Brain **fog**"
Sounds kind of romantic
I guess
But...
What was I saying?

*

First and last date:
She proclaimed
The bar's din
Made her feel
Deft

*

Times were I'd play
Eventide busk
Music's gone
I'm naught but a **husk**

*

My blood **circulates**
Doing its job

Continuously
Singing for you
As it toils

*

Shady Claire
Plethora of umbrellas
Hide her hair
Shhh: she's bald under there

*

Sometimes
Living
Is the hardest choice
Nevertheless
We wake
Knowing there is
Beauty

*

Suddenly
It's been forty years
Since 1980
And
The earth's **turbulence**
Wakes you

*

Your cold words
Wrap around my heart
The **condensation**
Cools my burning face

@JBeanHibbs

I find
Your voice,
Ever
Murmuring
In my thoughts,
Whispers of the heart

*

Galvanized nails
Lock my heart in place
Though I struggle
To
Abandon
Love

*

Quondam feelings
Come back
To life,
Through plump kisses,
That
Leave me
Breathless

*

These words
I scrawl
Won't free me,
Always
A
Hostage
To my
Demons

*

We remain
Scattered
Like dust
Over the plain,
Particles once joined
Now drifting

*

Love **propels**
My restless heart,
Through an ocean
Of anxiety,
To find peace

*

Stab my heart

Inject it
With love

Leave me a scar
To
Remember

*

In **deft** strokes,
You
Paint,
A story
To fill
This page,
Of us

*

We ponder
What will be,
As **efflorescence**
Pushes love,
Into our open
Hands

ⒶCT_FIRELIGHTS

Prelude ambience
to eternal sin
lips glossed
with liquid envy
burlesquing **panache**…

      *

Suspended reverie
in waning blush
Melting moonlight
scribing liquid dreams
in poetry…

      *

Skirting
blades of **fret**
in her tempest spirit
Brazen wings of silence…

*

Twisted tales
echo in hollow notes
with subzero woe
concealing the **punch**...

*

Indent bass pitches
striking
wicked ballads
as I summon
methodical
bohemian trance...

*

Release the lucid flow
and **salvage** harmony
casting magical connections
in rhapsody...

*

She speaks
in silent rain
exposing
a torn heart
to saltwater blades…

*

Time exposes
the luring moon
tracing **intangible**
golden light
with her secrets…

ⓐTBLEND3

Your eyes took
Away
The grit in my soul
Floral notes in lace

*

It was **askew**
My life
The sunset stole
a soul
It was mine

*

Clouds react in air **afar**
to your presence
Conceal incantations
of your smile

*

The **imposter** in my soul
Works hard
at whatever you choose
Select carefully

*

Concepts **becoming** fretted
strategic lies escape
carved in curfews
Death
has no border.

*

Trump's pilot fish
Swam **along**
Ate his ectoparasites
Then expelled
them to us

*

Her sips were **cautious**
His eyes were not
Their purview
Was her future

*

Love lost in the **woods** as
Crushed brown leaves
after a wind storm

*

The grammar of **fog**
Clinging wet goosebumps
Tempt a want
To be dry

*

haggle with the wind
It might work
If the sun
Was your ally

*

Your **feverish** touch
Rubs through my essence
Eye darts shot
I'm home now

@WINGEDWRITER90

The **waterway** had cleansed away my past sins,
But still the stars knew.

*

I **suspend** my heart
above my brains,
Foolery are ones engrossed in love.

*

My eyes **broaden**
Mouth waters
The delectable fae foods
Enticing with every scent

ⓐNADKIM

My soul became a **bookend**, forever observing and thus preserving knowledge from within.

*

Circulate the poison through my veins, make sure it gets beneath and destroys.

*

You used my **vertebrae** as a step ladder, but I pushed you away.

*

Explore the **corridor** of my life, see for yourself what I'm made of.

*

How **restless** am I, as my eyes take in the midnight sky tonight.

*

A **seafarer** drifts alone on the sea, all is lost, tired is he.

*

Accentuate the parts of yourself that meet the stars, where darkness meets light.

*

Even death could not **pacify** her thirst for knowledge or passion for life.

*

being me has never been easy, I carry my burdens like extra wings.

*

The **trapdoor** wasn't in the floor, it consumed my mind so long ago.

*

Shred my life, that I might see the shards that will forever remain.

*

My life is **askew**, full of shattered dreams, faded memories and split seams.

*

Death had a **reverence** for life, although she was the end, she smiled.

*

My **apotheosis** is coming, until then I shall drag myself along the way.

*

Enmesh me among the tattered pages of my life, leave me to sleep.

*

Retrieve the memories I once had, I'll be glad to have them back.

*

Piecing the parts of my life into a messy **collage** broken tiles.

@ThatLousyNick

Moonlit canyon
Holds
Unknown vectors

Possibilities

So
Damn
Hypnotizing

Okay

Consider me
Enchanted

*

Sunset crown
Accentuates

The magic in her eyes

Let's absquatulate

And
Chase starlight

*

Rivers flow
Alone

Through timescapes
Bleeding
Captured moments

But rivers
Coalesce

Why rush?

*

A life
In one **rucksack**

No trauma
Just drifting
Beautifully blind

Let's bounce

*

It's not you

We're all
Imposters

You're so close
Don't give up

Okay?

*

Feeling the words

Hashtag people
Craft

Veritable wonders

With
Archaeological obsession

Expect **turbulence**

ⒶFULLER_EDWARD

I
put
wing suit arms
out
streamlined
for **aerodynamics**
diving
into
controlled
abandon.

*

I didn't chase dreams.
I toiled with emptiness,
from fear of becoming **penniless**.

@DKMARIEAUTHOR

The **restless**
winter winds
of her frozen heart
wrap around your
summer love

       *

My maculate
Nomad heart
Found a home
And happiness
In your **immaculate** love

       *

You **interfere**
with my yesterdays
and todays

Please continue
with all my
tomorrows

*

The changing colors
of the season
catapults us
into the arms
of winter

*

Ditch **caution**
   Kiss me here
    Yes, right there
     If you dare
To answer my prayer

*

In the deep **woods**
amongst the fallen
scarlet and golden leaves
she dreams

*

I'm **tumultuous**
So very obstreperous
Difficult to control
But please just hold
Me

*

My foolish desires
Hold me **hostage**
Even as my wild
Heart   breaks
    Free

*

I'm a **husk**
Nostalgic
For your kiss
I miss
Your touch
So much

*

These **entanglements**
Of limbs and love
Wrap around hearts
Clutching passion
Embracing devotion

@CALLMECHEL_324

I pack up
  Feelings
    In **boxes**
      And some
    Haven't
    Been opened
For years

*

My nomadic spirit
Wanders the earth
Searching for another
Immaculately kindred with mine

*

How is it, my dear

    That even from **afar**

        Your glow is blinding?

*

The mirror

   Is my biggest

Haggler

   We argue

On what

   This reflection's worth

               *

Scribbled whispers

Are the **soliloquies**

Of my heart

Will you listen to them?

               *

You stripped my petals
Tore them to **shreds**
Leaving a naked
He-loves-me-not flower

               *

Our memories

Are just a **collage**

Of meldrops & tears

Across my pillow

                                                                       *

Alone
  We're just
    Shattered

     P
      i
       e
        c
       e
        s

Together
  Our **fragments**
    Collaborate
      To make
        Something beautiful

@HyKuWriter

where love meets hatred
one sees the river **frothing**
before it lays still

*

caught in a **loop**
he seduced a woman
before realizing
he needed improvements

*

to make her **glisten**
you have to simply listen
for what she desires

*

she **sifts** through a sieve
sugar on pecan sandies
known as mom sprinkles

*

to be of good cheer
sprinkle love generously
on those you hold dear

                *

what the wealthy fear
sitting upon the top **tier**
is to trickle tears

                *

i need to be fed
so i **graze** on fertile fields
reading poetry

                *

before it is **swept**
we discern how the tale ends
enjoy the journey

                *

master of the **woods**
declares his rule of the dark
the moon testifies

*

that long pause between
each kiss we speak with our eyes
rapturous delight

*

prisons without walls
dampen the soul's wings of flight
fear holds us **hostage**

*

deep within your cage
with every freedom fueled thrust
i **scatter** my rage

*

to **haggle** the price
exchanging dreams for false gold
means selling your soul

@AlanVMichaels

Morning dew
filled my heart
Thoughts of you
couldn't part our
foggy sea

    *

footprints
the only mark
of my earthly existence
swept away
by insouciant tides

    *

When you realize
we are **fragments**

of
exploding
stars

it transforms
your consciousness

*

Never look for
quantum **entanglements**
with a lonely alien
in a space bar

*

Birth is just step one
in a string of lessons for
becoming human

*

I've lived
too **cautiously**
It's time
to change that
before
it's too late

*

A lonely beauty
a gilded cage
the fab life
forever self-ensconced
jailbird screeching

*

Amelia searches
from the widow's walk
praying her **seafarer**
returns to her arms

*

I am your
hostage
I need
your love
to survive
I submit
completely

*

It's pretty simple:

Horses sweat
Men perspire
Women **glisten**

Don't get it twisted!

@JoyPainLoveWrit

You are a **sprinkle**
of effervescent
stardust on the
cupcake of my life

*

We shall meet again
across lifetimes and
lost love letters,
Searching for soul

*

Autumn is a striking
collage of colours
bursting out of summer's
green monochrome

*

Sifting through broken shells,
with cuts on my fingers,
looking for a pearl

*

As her soul
shattered
beyond **retrieve**,
She kept smiling,
eyes watery,
lips curved

*

His eyes
widened
over her **deft**
perceptions,
She sees love
in him...how?

*

T'was serendipity,
This love, this adoration,
Souls **enmesh**,
Hearts a flutter,
Forever ever

*

It was an uphill battle,
reaching the **apotheosis**
of love, ego be damned

*

I feel the pull
of this **hiraeth**,
towards the sea,
towards the sunset

*

I **shred** these
memories to pieces,
and let the wind
blow them away

*

Fill this broken heart
and **replenish** this
parched soul with
love so intoxicating

④COCOESSENCES

your verses, — flowers
flowers **advocate** for butterflies
butterflies pollinate love
love is you

*

he **entrusted** his heartbeats
in alluring poems... —
également
tapestried my beauty in them

*

he's not kissing me... —
he savors my essence's **particles**, —
a marvelous physical story...

*

ingredients of my smiles, —
deliciously **bombardment**, —
a mentholated velvety fudge
nourishing you, instantly

*

some expect attentions
even if **nevertheless**
they never appreciated
something shared by you

*

trusting in readers discretion
we expose **galvanizing** words,
[in—ti—mate—ly]… some
guarantee maximum intensity

*

a thought
activates my emotions

my emotions **punch**
straight in your heart

Intelligently

*

steps of my thoughts dance
thru the metaphors' mosaic
with you…sentimental **visitor**

*

even if someone froze my posts,
comments… whatever…
restless, my time explores you…

*

the miracle of music
surrounds earth

stretching itself
entertains you

like kitten does

*

mirabelle and cherry bloomed…
mixture crystalline **efflorescence**
circulate back and forth
infusing sophistication

④SCRIBBLED_LINES

whispering winds
murmuring rivers
roaring waves
beats of hearts
all crooning
      single anthem.

      *

Becoming a champion
despite **successive** knockouts,
a true spirit
on which world runs.

      *

Their scars **pacify**, nullify
each other
permitting light to heal,
 love to bloom

      *

Immerse in my
　meandering love
　my darling ,
　evolving from it
　an eternal impossibility.

＊

entanglements,
the source of tattoos
on heart
narrating tales of
separation and sunsets

＊

Through the **fog**

of midnight,

he set sail from

my heart to hers.

＊

ransack the altar
freeing rejection
and recluse
resurrect paradise
revelling in the now

*

If future plans **askew**
Then courage, resilience
My cord brothers,
Rise will I.

*

bleeding petals
lotus dew
bubbles in waves
cavorting does
mortal men
all **being**

*

Facing the bleeding Sun
swaying, shy in amber shade
beatific Daffodils **entertain** Bees

@DrGeetaBhandari

Mesmerised
by
his
panache,
heart
goes
roller
coaster,
mind
awestruck,
the
being
reincarnated.

Efflorescence
of
his
passion
seeped
into
my
porous
heart,
dissolving ,
mingling
blooming
love.

*

In
market
of
desires
demand
unlimited,
supply
too
unlimited,
no
customers
for
satisfaction.

(A)JOYENZED

Her soul
flies **afar**
from the
hospital bed
farewelling
all she holds dear

*

Surreptitious dementia
stalked the minds
of her prey
Altering, **pacifying**,
finally stealing away

*

She wears despair
with ethereal **panache**
Dressing in vintage grief
for him, always.

*

Magnetic attraction
of stardust within us
Our **fragments**
irresistibly drawn
in heavenly collaboration

*

Is there laughter
in the hereafter?
Or a purgatory
with no mirth **anymore**?

*

Braided rivers
of tears
unraveling
Wearing winter blues
as her measure
of sorrow

*

A heart's the size
of a closed fist.
One gives,
one receives,
punches.

*

Your plump lips curved
around my soul
feel like I'm **being**
swallowed whole

*

Don't **fret**,
my muse
whispers silently,
I won't be gone
for too long.

*

Your **whirlwind** nature
leaves a trail
of shattered dreams
behind
when you leave

@MarshaWritesIt

ransack me like a knapsack
where everything you need
is in the bottom

*

tear open the wrapping
overturn the **boxes**
maybe Christmas
spirit will drop out

*

I **immerse** my uncertainties
in mocha foam
and like tiny marshmallows
they float

*

desire needles me
I wake from dreams of last nights
murmuring their names

*

patience brings solace
to the **countless** hours
between the end
and the beginning

        *

I'm gifted
I can hit my
own head
with a skillet
and **panache**

        *

no yearling amour **anymore**
muscle melted and reborn
as mutual comfort
and armour

        *

I **haggle** with the mirror
trading smiles for lines
and bargaining for acceptance

        *

I take solace
in a single kiss
encumbered by years
outweighing **countless** tears

*

a **visitor**
made it through
my deadened maze
to deliver a welcome smile

*

tangled limbs form
limbic **entanglements**
endocrine streams
sway dopamine rushes
we remember love

*

a woman's work is never done
internet history **swept** clean
mind still dirty

@KEMWRITING

She wonders at nimble thoughts
and agile movement
how **deft** they dance together

*

Dragonflies dart about
hover as butterflies
and flowers
dance in
summer's breeze
Magical

*

Her smile, a mask
Her laugh, a lie

Her truth
surreptitious
and deadly

*

She strains her soul
sifts it for worth
in glittering specks
of moments

     *

I wish to **graze**
on your passing days
live inside
your burning eyes

     *

A **couple** words
A brief touch

I am yours
And
You are mine

     *

I wish to
accompany
lost loves
into Death's realm

*

glistening tears
buried too long
emerge
from their refuge
and devastate
emotional states

*

Quondam desires
dwindled
like embers
put out
before barren eyes
under darkening
skies

ⓐIRIEPOETRY

while rejecting the illusion
of an **immaculate** love
i savor intimacy's
serene authenticity

*

like a bee's sweet **elixir**
i quench my thirst with
your honeyed words

*

positive **perception** of our feedback loop remained
then deceit surpassed its tipping point

*

his melodic aspect
projects a prosodic inflect
as i experience intense **rhapsodic** effect

*

skill of his pen
stardust without end
lost in a **prism**
magnetic vision

*

earth's **bounteousness**
a source of light heat and change
the magma bursts forth

*

i no longer speak
you no longer listen
silent **canyons**
deepen over time

*

i prefer science
one hundred percent
over **divine** office
and its blinding intent

*

like **Galileo**'s telescope
a sky filled with your stars
is all i hope

*

hubris
ignores good intention
tangles us
in ongoing deception
simply by
altering perception

***unravelling**

*

the distance between
his need and my surrender
is measured with
one growl

***countless**

⑭TsukiakariUsagi

⌈The **restless** mind,
   always there, nagging;
     sometimes good,
       sometimes bad;
  forever We're resilient.⌋

*

⌈**Campfires** burn low,
  while Stars glitter on high.
•
•
•
Cassiopeia jealously watches
  the Princesses.⌋

*

⌈A busy **market**,
  a sea of grey,
    there You were ~
   colourful.
   beautiful.
   resplendent. ⌋

⁎

⌈My heart
    - no longer **galvanised** -
      sits, rusting in the rain,
        scattered...
       useless...
        broken.⌋

⁎

⌈Rain falls softly upon the meadow,
Her naked skin **glistens** with each drop.⌋

⁎

⌈These damned **entanglements**...
emotions... logic...
    ~ Happiness;
      ~ Sadness;
   ~ Loneliness;
    ~ Fear;
E-X-H-A-U-S-T-E-D!
  ~ Survivor.
Always forward.⌋

⁎

⌈Loving from **afar**,
　　distantly kept —
　　　　clutching futility to hope —
　　　　　　slipping…
　　　　　　　　…
　　　　　　　…
　　　　　　…
　　　　　…
　　　　finally letting go.⌋

　　　　　*

⌈Vivid memories,
　　ransacked hearts…
　　　　once full of love,
　　　　　　— now broken —
　　　　　　　　strewn carelessly about.⌋

　　　　　*

⌈These **fragments** of memories —
　　they haunt me —
　　　　unable to connect the pieces —
　　　　　　Trauma.⌋

(A)WhiskeySourHour

tiny fingers **scatter**
wildflower seeds
atop eager soil and
yearn for the spring

*

breathless and
tangled
our bodies **glisten**
glow
and moan
piled between your sheets

*

emotional **haggling**,
weighing pros, cons,
affections against dejection—
of letting you back in

*

he **ransacks** the archives
of his psyche
when i ask what
he feels

*

Unlace your death grip from my throat and let me
come into **being**

*

reaching into my pocket, feeling only **fragments** of
what was—
it's not enough

*

maybe my thrashing will
summon the tide
to tow me back to shore

*

shroud your trembling fingers
and smile when cued—
the **imposter** sharpens her tools

*

endless batting,
swatting, swiping —
the **cautious** rain
as repentant
as she is wet

*

heart found rib-bound,
fists **sequestered**
behind my yearning spine
begging you
for release

*

i won't look back
at us **fondly**,
instead, i'll look
to the side

(A)MOOMOOSEUM

The waves came in

And the waves went out

Just like love,

Nevertheless.

*

I penned **bounteous** letters,

Stood on them until my head touched the moon.

*

We watch the gibbous moon

Effusing handfuls of seeds

That grow into stars.

*

The **plethora** of clouds have spilled everywhere on the ground,

Just like popcorn

*

Each incision

Into the **canyons** of your soul

Echoes of a bleeding heart.

*

Listen to her **soliloquy**

Accordion waves, threshing

Against the sky of your mouth

*

Winter was **feverish**

Until she put her loving arms around the setting sun.

*

He grieved the **deft** touch of her lips upon his lips,

The apocalypse

*

For us,

You tore the **husk** from the sky

To begin another world

*

S T A R S
_____

When you threw the seeds up into the sky
They turned to **glitter**

*

Between the stubborn peaks of
their souls,

The iceberg weeped its frigid
forgiveness.

⑷ FHAEDRA

Mornings

Stretch out

Gaze while breathing

Reach

Open wide

Sprinkle new light

Abide

      *

Draw your shades
What you see
Sways decisions
Listening overrides
Merely **optical** impressions

      *

Black pots sit empty on the patio.
Ravens **circulate** rumours.
Trees shed.
Autumn.

*

There it is

exposed

Deep obscenity

Smiling portrait
We killed him
Headlines bellow

*

Approach mine

If you dare

Your **thievery** robs your own soul

Fading shadow

*

Across sunflower fields

Beyond poplar groves

A passenger train's whistle

calls for you.

*

Blue Dot Inhabitants

Our

Collective legacy

Elevated evolvers

Frivolous **fragments** or

Flawed fallacy

*

I poet mime words
Sentiment muted
Imposter stamped
Across these lips
of time

@ANNABURNSWRITES

And yet
I have lived
Countless lives
Finding solace
In none of them

*

World nomad on an
Immaculate journey
Searching realms to
Find pieces of me

*

Collaborate with me
Creating dreamscapes
Of remembrance
Forming our chapters
From only **fragments**

*

Sun petals **visit**
On a gentle wind
Whispering your name
Through mosaic skies

*

Waxing moon
Scatters her
Transcendent text
The sea and sky
Scribed in light

*

You made me crawl on
Carpets of broken glass
And **shredded** flower petals

*

Hope lives here
If only to overturn
These little **boxes**
That contain us

*

Do we still wish for
Passions reborn

For we don't really
Talk **anymore**

*

Evening spirit **beckons**
A watermelon sunset
Trickling across the sky
Into deeper blues

*

Unravel velvet universes
Soft measures of time
And still he feels
Like home

*

Forget **quondam** glories
And together we will
Render the genesis
Of new memories

(A)MARK_NIFICENT

As a creation of joy,
perfect happiness is your
natural state of **being**

*

Despite lack of attention
love is freely
given without
expectation or obligation
nevertheless.

*

Crescendo of violet,
shimmering twilight,
even darkness harbours light.

Brightness can not die.

*

Your song reverberates
in my heart **everlong** -
dance of love and
thanksgiving eternal.

*

The Lord is my shepherd
I may safely **graze**
without danger or harm.

*

From the **entanglement**
of our **particles** -
a quantum tunnel
to love is born.

*

Genesis of this poem
started after
reading your words -
eloquent song of angels.

*

There is no gap
so wide,
chasm so deep
faith cannot leap
across.

*

Ransacking
adagios of her body,
he found the right places
to please her.

*

Upon dense **woods**,
one spark is
all it takes
to start a fire.

*

Out of your smile,
magnetic pulse hits the heart -

I am in love.

Another take at it coming straight out of your poem.

@PATRICI30730227

In a **rucksack**
full of memories
there's always room
for one more

You…

*

An **orchestra** of memories
playing inside my mind
nostalgic chords
of longing songs

*

You **retrieved** life
from my body
while you taught me
how to die

*

My heart patched
became a **collage**
of the memories
I have of you

          *

I walk alone
but the footprints
of your words
accompany the steps of mine

          *

Your **fluttered** words
ripples in my heart
ravaged agape
that torn it apart

          *

Thorns on flesh
bleeding in misery
traces of you
that time cannot **erode**

          *

Looked up
One wish
and
a **couple** of stars later
I'm still waiting…

*

You are the **visitor**
that when comes back
feels like you never left

*

If I had been **cautious**
my heart would
not have lost
its beat

*

It was not **thievery**.
I gave him the key
to open my heart

ⓐFAXTORS

She never needed a knife
She had her words
To **stab** his hearts

*

There is nothing else left **anymore**
Words and poetry
Reason for being alive

*

Countless possibilities
But if we don't take that risk, we will never know

*

Words **scattered**
Heart shattered
Feelings unfeathered
Consequences of your name
Being always uttered

*

Nothing else matters but
Being alive matters
Being happy matters
Being you matters

*

Some words **entertain**
Some words relate
Some are just expressions
Some words heal

*

Being **cautious**
He started writing
His words entertained none
He wrote for himself

*

Restless mind wandering around thoughts
Without doubt it starts overthinking
Killing all thoughts

*

She held his heart **hostage**
Until she was done playing and hurting him

*

I can only feel myself
When I **immerse** myself in your beautiful soul

*

Words don't matter **anymore**
Actions don't matter anymore
Silence stabs harder

*

She tore him apart
Making **countless** pieces of his heart
Still in love

*

That **restless** feeling
It's so common now
Every night it returns with rains

*

Instead of freeing her soul
His love **suffocated** her
Making her soul loveless

ⓐHILLSIS

I open my heart
but
why do people
keep giving
it a **punch**?

*

My mind
being restless
You **pacify** me
with soothing words
and comforting actions

*

Our bodies
glisten with sweat
from making love
endlessly
in this squeaky bed

*

I lived in a **fog**
When suddenly
you appeared
and the clouds
dissipated

*

When our pheromones clash,
particles of passion and love
whizz around our bodies

*

We do not
need to **haggle**
Our love
for each other
is priceless

*

I watch you
from **afar**
With each step
you come closer
I smile

*

My world is **askew**
You reach your gentle hand
and pick me up

*

Please
take me **hostage**.
I give you
my body,
mind,
heart
and
Soul.

*

I
was a **quondam** failure
But you believed
and we traveled towards
success

@THEEDEMURAH

gazing
at the stars

thinking
of the reasons
I love you

both
countless

        *

Newton struck
holds apple offender
and ponders

Seafarer fears edge
loses hope
wanders

        *

Sinking into your verse
full **immersion**

I am now your disciple
complete conversion

*

future **boxed**
in cardboard

tears torrential
dissolving

hope's entropy
dissipates

expanding universe
grows colder

*

Dear Cupid,

please return
your aim's fine

I dodge well

Sincerely,
exposed Heart

*

snow **drifts**
thoughts astray

your golden skin
summer's day

heated memories
tucked away

                *

confessing love
hope travels

seeing you
throat constricts
gravels

all my cool
Unravels

                *

Carrying you along
with my yesterdays

Wishing I could see you
in my tomorrows

(4) SERENE_SHE

He started
Avoiding her
When he
Was unable to
Resist even her
Condensed thoughts.

*

Neither his
Stubbornness
Nor her
Argument
Could **erode**
Their love
Everytime
Turned
Strong.

*

With you
Chaos is calm
Without you
Calm is chaotic
Restlessness is **restless**.

*

In my thoughts
In my solitude
I would love
You to
interfere anytime.

*

Their romantic
interlude
Once again proved
Love gives fairytale
Amidst our busy lives.

*

Sparkling Eyes
Broad Smile
Are reflection
Of every **eons**
That your Love
Showers.

*

Amongst my chaos
His presence comes
As a **waft** of
Serenity and sublimity.

*

In spite of
Glory
She only
Craved for
His **bounteous**
Love and attention.

*

Things left
Unattended
Gets worse.
The wound,
Pain , Love
Even the
Leaking **faucet**

@SOMAXDATTA

hear the world
diminish leaving
only the prickle
of my breath
salty air

*

end of days
locusts descend after the
sand storms and death plagues

*

Waves crashing below
My tilted wing
Froth cresting
Aquamarine surges
From ocean's floor

*

Note by note
black and blue
the greatest pain
as her worth
erodes

*

MoonFlower beckons.
Your gentle approach isn't
necessary.
My petals come
backed with steel.

@EdHaiku575

Early morning dew
Grass **glistens**
Songbirds melody
Softly announce
Daylight bleaches
Dark night

*

Pen
Propels
Her ink
Giving birth
To words
Blank sheet
In ecstasy
Absorbs

*

Poetry isn't about
The right words
But
How light is felt
They **scatter**

*

Butterflies frolicking
Quondam cocoon
Crumbles
While my
Behavioral straitjacket
More
And more
Stripes

*

Abandoned
Living in **boxes**
Experience an
Unknown warmth
After snuggle up
To myself

*

Our carving
In tree's bark
Becomes
A scar
While the **fog**
Gets denser

*

Advocate patience
To listen and
Wait
Some more
To hear
Trying
To tell

*

All darkness will treasure
Absorption
Of virgin white light
When your moon rises

*

There is a forest
Getting lost
Because **unravelling**
Gives
Too many ways out

(A) TALWAI SARITA

Sift through
The polished grains of words.
The chaff has a story too.

*

A **surreptitious** memory
That sneaks in
Like a dark cloud
Threatening to rain.

*

One man's calm
Is another's storm.
A ripple,
Tumultuous wave
To a leaf.

*

Grandiloquence
Is just **froth**
Disguised as coffee.
Do not get stimulated by it.

*

A gamut of sensations
Between the vaporisation
And the **condensation**
Of that dreaded emotion.

*

Encourage
Curiosity in children
And they will forever be **irreverent**
To holy cows.

*

Turn your **rifled** memories
Into potpourri.
Place them in the folds
Of time.

*

Life always finds a way
A **cleft** in the cobbles
And grass shoots.

*

An **optical** illusion,
When you see love
Or hate
Where there is none.

*

I walk
And write
And bake
And paint
But still my **faucet** leaks.

*

The law
Of diminishing returns
Plays out through life
Diminish
Or be **diminished**.

*

I sprout new leaves
From thorns and roots
An abundant **foliage**
Surrounds me.

(4)NCSCRAWLS

saltwater
mists her face
briny **froth** trawls
a skin that no longer fits

*

Urashima unlatches
her tortoiseshell coffer,
turbulence bends his spine
into a circumvented century

*

He **ditched** me
in a diner
at a crossroads
between universes
—none mine.

*

My **rifle** renders
perfect crosshairs on my face
crossed time to end me

*

What way would digital I
transcend the physical being that
I am not?

*

Like a snail's eye
my heart's **cautious** extrusion
cringes inward
at your touch

*

I **unravel**
my fears
into your care
you neatly plait them
into garlands

*

I **sift** through
shrine grains
tuck rice
into tofu pockets
lure gingery foxes

*

a running **soliloquy**
attends my days,
at times
interrupted
by conversations of expediency

*

I reach for
the **afterglow**
of his touch...
my fingers close
on gloaming

@MELJ_WRITES

No matter
how one **haggles**
with the mirror,
2020's haggard face
stares back.

*

Teardrops **glisten**
 on a weathered face,
a mournful melody plays,
death lingers, listens.

*

The price of sex
is steep -
a broken heart
to reap,
galvanize yourself.

*

Can you measure
unraveling hearts
when the ties that bind
are worlds apart?

*

Charming **imposter**
heart's dreary lament,
disregarded portent
believed false content,
sorrows were fostered.

*

Rumors **bombard**
with fabricated
whispers

wounded soul's cry
as others laugh;
heart's scarred.

*

Hearts **afar**
trust lapsed
soul laid bare
love didn't last,
oversimplified -
we're past.

*

Despair
has no **panache** -
it's quiet,
without flare
it hides behind
smiling mirages.

*

Cluttered mind
filled, struggling
like a packed
box overturned,
seeking clarity
finding disparity.

ⒶMILA255H

I am haunted by the memory of my own **being**
Nightmares overwhelm deeply

@MariaAPerez1

I looked at the mirror
Studied my face
That is not me
Anymore

*

No surprise
Your **countless** lies
How selfish
To drag us down
With you

*

The palm trees sway
Rambunctious waves play
Wild winds slay
A hurricane day

*

Penniless but proud
    Each word a treasure
Measured by
    A dream come true

*

Your words
Will not **diminish** me
I am a jewel in the rough

*

Entanglements
Around the White House
What for?
To Keep In
Or
Keep Out?

*

Each word, a **punch**
Meant to strike me down
No use, I'm stronger

*

Stay **away**
Doubt and Fatigue
Get out of my way
Insecurity
Winning today

⑭ THE LADY MAGIC

Beneath
brilliant
blue moon,
sepia owl
flies **along**
between
ink silhouettes
of trees.

*

Little me
opened store's
cage doors.
"Fly free,
little ones -
**jailbirds
no more.**"

*

We were his
mosaic entourage -
always
dressed to the nines,
smiles,
and **panache**.

*

Pines condemned
by greedy
haggling
paper company
lacking
introspection
shown
within
icy reflections

@LeahBordreaux2

Our eyes meet in the rearview,

and there we are

sequestered in miniature.

*

Sleep,
tiny **seafarer**,
dreamer of dreams.
Tomorrow can keep its troubles.
Tonight drift.

*

Once in my
T
  R
    A
      P
        DOOR mind

thoughts never escape,

merely scramble my frantic brain.

*

It is utter peace

to ignore a world

that seeks endlessly

to **entertain**.

*

Ah, that **jailbird** smile,
cages my heart,
makes it stutter and flutter so

*

Saw that glint in your eyes,

knocked my halo **askew**.

Somehow, you knew.

*

Shyly, we **immerse** ourselves in tasks of love.

The universe watches, breathless.

*

From particles we come together.

A
Cosmic
Dance

Into **particles** we fly apart.

*

I am
held
hostage
by
the bits
of you
that
capture
my soul.

*

Our smitten hearts,

like children in the **woods**,

run 'round in raucous delight.

ⓐKrypticKro

~

shelves were **askew**
with old magic books covered in dust;

such a paradise...

~

*

~

winds blowing
golden leaves so **restless**
seeking sanctuary
from this
approaching cold season...

~

*

~

spectrums unimaginable
begin amidst a **plethora** of widespread
changes, within our every season..

~

*

~
leaves in
a **tumultuous**
escapade, dancing
in autumn winds
across
empty harvest fields..
~

*

~
turning a quiet darkness
into something that **glistens**
like kisses on your lips..
~

*

~

breath
blending together..

this **feverish** compulsion
reaches
slow beneath
your cover of darkness..

~

*

~

no way to
keep
star clusters
from **interfering** further..
comets now
carried us...

~

@WDIBarry

she turns the skies
into **shreds**

& from the pieces
weaves her soul

       *

the **lissome** poetics
of fragmented fractals

only entangled loners
fit into pointe shoes

       *

she smiles a **turbulence**
the winds blow
waters rise

I

fall

in love

*

the prophet
chases salvation
through abnegation

the poet
catapults upward
with a word

*

an obstreperous
silence

a **tumultuous**
presence

I remember her kisses
delicious & dangerous

*

an **immaculate** smile
from a stranger

abandoned

a jewel comported
for my camera

*

in a
canyon
of words
there is
only one
way out
turn   write

*

caged

faucet
streaming
forest sounds
onto blank papers
catching birds upon
po
et
ry

uncaged

⑷ByThisWillAlone

wrens feign interest
tilt heads as in **reverence**
to the scratch of words

*

machines press the oars
row the **seafarer** ast tides
in far cosmic voids

*

in the way my hands
rest atop a **plethora**
of lonesome street noise

*

from here to that
corner, maybe the turnpike
i'll **haggle** for sensible curses

*

at peace with lament
solitude with willow
provisionary
divulging pretended swords
disassembled **afterglow**

*

you **retrieve** lavender
only once
just a suggestion
of departed scent
distant passengers

*

fogged window
scored by multifarious fingers
the **froth** of exhalation
renews the canvas

*

obsess in measure
when cicadas raise
a fractal evening chant
of seasoned **turbulence**

*

i stopped when
 the clocks stopped
  arresting **lissome** digits
   in lieu of
    sleeping

*

and i will sit proud
 gather **fragments** into
  a collaborate engine
  made desire

*

write a single word into **being**
 prevaricate
 stare, whistle, hum
 open blank page

*

the revelers **effuse**
 shouting abandon
 skipping stone after stone
 while building such poems

@LOVERNO87785276

My love for you
Crept up,
Like a ninja assassin.
A welcome **visitor**?

*

You know it's love when you feel **satiated** after just seeing their face.

*

Discarding artist's brushes
Entrust instead
Her bringing
Natural curves.
Deep strokes
Creating memories.

*

gathering up
shattered pieces
lying,
scarred,
on frozen earth,
to somehow **salvage**,
hope

*

Navigating this friendship
Is a complicated
Joyous
Painful
Heartfelt
Mindfuck
Teasing
Love
Necessity?

@HayleyReeseChow

I plucked splinters
of infected memories,
and
  scattered
    my
       ashes
          to
             the
                wind.

*

Stained glass windows
emblazoned **particles** of universe,
dancing to the hum of time.

*

We raced raindrops down **windowpanes**,
the sky reminding us it's okay to cry.

*

Unminded,
Time's **crabgrass** overgrew their friendship,
Another garden lost in weeds of silence.

*

He stole into my dreams,
and we danced the night away,
Two **somnambulists**.

*

The **bounteous** leaves rained down,
dying embers of another blazing summer
gone cold.

*

Surrendering,
she plunged through
midnight soaked skies,
into the
endless **efflorescence**
of stars.

*

Her heart crumpled,
She replaced it with tempered steel.
Heavy,
But not **disposable**.

*

Our love is one blink
amid starry **eons**,
but still,
it consumes me.

*

She longs to be alone,
but the loneliness **accompanies** her
wherever she goes.

*

They crashed together,

repercussions shattering

two glassy futures

to build one

enduring passion.

④WEITWRITE

Memory in **fragments**
A green fern
A ray of sun
A holiday ramble

*

Ransacking the shopping sites
Looking for the perfect gift.
Why does my heart hurt?

*

Wrapping **boxes**, easy
Hand knit scarves, harder
Just give me gift bags, please!

*

Frosted blue eye shadow
Cinched pale yellow satin waist
The 60's **glistened** change

*

The uncle in stretched t-shirt
And rummy breath
Arrives.
Unwelcome **visitor**.
"Come in!"

*

The cheque was refused
At the grocery store
We were **penniless**
Again!
Despair!

*

Quondam
Friend
Your drama
Exhausts me
Your story
An endless loop
Of him

*

Wild geese **galvanize**
To fly in a perfect V
The heron deep throats
Solitude

*

Feverish with excitement
Pumped by weeks of preparation
They expect her to sleep!

*

Practice the art of **haggling**
No, Mom. They're poor.
My daughter, the teacher

*

Anymore
Related to everyone
Everywhere
Wondering how anything
Will survive
Wait!
Anytime now.

ⓐLRHudgins

Einstein's theories
About time and space
Were an early chapter in
quondam physics.

*

An errant sunbeam
highlights frantic dust **particles**
as they perform
the danse macabre

*

We believe the media even when they haven't got a **shred** of evidence.

*

Crystal clear **lagoon**
Shelter from the raging storm
We drop sail and wait

*

Birth and death
Sit like **bookends**
On shelves filled with
your fondest memories

*

December
The last days of the **imposter**
The advent of a new hope

*

We **sift** through the sands
of time to uncover layers of archaeological
mysteries

*

After a snowfall
We'd **traipse** through forests,
Hunting for galax
Shooting at mistletoe.

*

This year brought zombie minks and murder
hornets. Still waiting for the punchline

@PALLAVI31

after being
swallowed,
regurgitated
by the void,
she emerges
 as pure
galvanized
awareness

*

unshed tears **glisten**
in his eyes, as she left,
drowning in her own

*

anything sells
in the transactional
market of pseudo
human entanglements,
instant gratification wins

*

the mind is an
imposter of
presumptions and
a predilection for
convenient truths

*

apotheosis of
living my life
would be to be
desireless with
active purpose

*

form or formless,
does not **diminish**,
absolute truth of
you residing in me

*

your **deft** way of
teasing me out of
my melancholy
melts my heart

*

the **restful** moon gleams,
blissfully unaware of,
yearning heartbeats of this
restless heart

*

random, floating words
with no actual meaning
stab deeply cutting
through the heart

*

entanglements,
we knowingly
get tangled in,
hoping to escape
the simplicity of
reality

DMDAVANTI

Silence,
that dark
collaborator
enables
sharp
fragments
of memories
to surface
come nightfall.

*

Stray
from the **campfire**
escape the calyx
and creature comforts
embrace the scare.

*

October sings
in flapping
bat wings
the **immaculate** shadow
of a
black cat.

*

Forced to
haggle
with static
 the
horror
of drowning
in your own
noise.

*

Shadows
are the
last safe
preserve
of the bone weary
and hopelessly
discarded.

*

Season in transit
cycle sweet
equinox
rainfall
to **accentuate**
the echo
of autumn.

*

With
celestial thoughts
she
ransacks
the stars
for the key
to the
universe.

*

Raw fury of
aesthetic so
desperately needed
to **retrieve**
all that's been lost.

*

Expecting a soiree
a scarlet path
welcomes
the **hostage**
to my
revenge machine.

@HEATH_LAWS

Try to **bookend**
each day as much
as possible with
laughter and inspiration

*

Left in awe
by heartfelt words
love shows **reverence**
for hope filled souls

*

Words **scatter**
sowing seeds of
knowledge while
hoping to reap
fields of inspiration

*

Strolling along the **promenade**
underneath an ebon sky
filled with heavenly
starlit dreams

*

Clouds cluster within
reach of withered hands
as **highlands** perch toward
the heavens

*

Love letters written
on windows as **condensation**
allows the language
of a poet

*

The scent of honeysuckle
began to **waft** through
the meadow that
summer afternoon

*

Heartbreak lessons
led his mind to
estrange his heart
to protect his soul

     *

An **interlude** between
heartbeats was
a pause to gather
the breath of love

     *

A beautiful **collage**
as the colors of nature
paint the canvas of earth

     *

Sitting **cliffside** as
sunset beauty falls
into the welcoming arms
of days end

@JPGarlandAuthor

The **orchestra** was loud
But I heard
The sweet melody
Of your piccolo.

*

The **crabgrass** stains
Along my pants
And shirt
Were proof of my
Infidelity.

*

They **scatter** before you
In fear
But I see
You have
No
Clothes.

*

My parents
Made me
Who I am,
Estrange me
For who I am.

*

The loss of **foliage**,
Leaves
Trees naked
As am I
Having lost
You.

*

I won't **haggle**
About my love.
I give it to you
Without
Conditions

*

A **sprinkle** here.
A sprinkle there.
In no time
You have
Love Ocean.

*

Sequester the jury
Disqualify the judge
Erupt in a fury
I won't budge.

*

She is a cruel queen,
Her **honeycomb** drips
With the rejecteds'
Wasted
Seed.

*

I was **swept** away
Not caring
That I
Was drowning
In your blood.

AMOSCHOENFELD

bullying…
the **punch** line
of a joke that isn't funny,
even decades later

*

soul **unravelling**
her children at each other's throats
hell on earth, pure failure

*

swept like autumn
leaves into a neat pile:
vulnerable hopes tempt rough winds.

*

entrusted with forgiveness
the stony earth absorbed remorse with compassion
midwife to rebirth

*

bronzed woods
singed by sunset,
salve to my aches
as darkness waits...

patiently.

*

dragging thread
across the decades
to mend this wrong...

clumsy stitching in knots.

*

restless stomach
p a n i c s !
refuses to settle
until self-sabotage
seduces with its false peace

*

glistening tears sting
cold fog bites, hitting bone
damp seeps into hidden vulnerability

*

guitar **campfire**
singing out the soul's beat
for beaten souls
finding their rhythm

*

menopausal mood dips
   propel the boat
backwards
  dropping
  anchor
while still in motion

*

enmeshed in empathy
the tendrils of tenderness
reached, enveloped, embraced
and transformed her

ⓐIpsaHerself

Punch drunk
on the libation of love
just requited--
you take another sip.

*

The body
is a **husk**
for the soul,
slowly shucked
by time's hand.

*

Will you **retrieve** me
from the unspeakable lengths
of the river without name?

*

A light-struck **exposure**
from a summer long ago--
only a golden silhouette remains.

*

Penniless
but dollar rich--
the dragon demands
the luckless profit
as a sacrifice.

*

kintsugi--
I sweep up
autumn's **scattered** leaves
and glue them on
gold branches

*

Ink **immersed** in water--
a thousand stillborn words
uncurl ghostly hands
and disperse.

*

The magpie's nest--
a **collage**
scavenged
for an egg
that was also scavenged.

*

Your eyes
are electric lights from which
an improbable color
effuses--
never blink.

*

Your lips quake.
My hands tremble.
Our bodies navigate
the **turbulence** of desire.

*

The birch
stretches skyward,
lissome
as the dryad
entombed
in her hollow heart.

@WHATSUPNOWHUN

None **sequester** sas thoroughly as words that needed saying but missed their say.

*

Rain smacking down as lightning bolts **punch** through atmosphere; violent yet perfectly cozy.

*

Cautious folks have forgotten that this is all make believe.
But not me.

*

Sodden **boxes**, wilting in the rain and waiting at the curb for goodbye.

*

He struts because souls crushed young are made impenetrable by grit and **panache**.

*

Apparently,
Holes like this fester.
Being without you,
Is harder than I imagined.

*

Beauty and sharp claws to **entertain** the eager,
toothy, grins those wild sorts sport.

*

I **entrust** my love tinged tears to solemnly
evaporate and join you there.

*

Fiddle, tickle and trace
Down her **robust** waist

Worshipping those curves
Especially hers

@SarikaJaswani

Eyes betray
Ears elude
Only heart sees, hears,
glistens to
melody of soul

*

Gale & a rose
scent of your name
genesis of a bond unbroken

*

Reality and dreams
dualism on train tracks
like **bookend** holds life
never meet

*

Agelast mirror
espies raised **vertebrae**
crossbow to the wrench of
isochronal time

*

She wore her
despair
like **panache** on
   A C O
  E   C
P & K
danced away
rain of pain

*

I've built mind walls
for credulous skyhigh
nevertheless your love
finds cracks to cascade springs

*

Between
stolen glances windows
& bold stares doors
walls of love confessions
lay **askew**

*

Conquered **highlands**
of senses, crawled
heart walls & made
room in your heart

*

Afterglow of sky
Helms me into the fog
Barefoot I amble
On clouds

*

Unspoken words
froth at corners of
lips that have chosen
to stay sealed

*

Autumn shiver
runs down spine,
face captures carmine hue
of fall **foliage** at first kiss

@COLINBEVIS1

A complicated web
she did weave though
its **unraveling** was a beautiful thing…

*

Merely a **visitor**
to her heart
till he realised
it was his home

*

Her sense of calm
always seemed
restored in the
tranquility within
ancient **woodlands**

*

Across stormy skies
lies the calm that is
her oh so beautiful soul

*

Countless times he
had walked the road
alone seeking
a mythical
forever home

*

Deserving
a romantic
interlude
they **sequestered**
themselves in
a cabin by the lake

*

Living like
a **jailbird**
imprisoned
by self doubt
Released by
her loving touch

*

No words from him
could **pacify**
her angst
so he kissed
her instead

*

His **restless** soul
so full of angst
found peace in
her loving arms

*

An **imposter**
haunts
my mind
Begone
oh dark one
let there be light

@DAVID_MCTIGUE

Imprisoned heart;
its' twin **jailbird**
incarcerated soul
awaits parole.

Remorseful.
Penitent.
Pending appeal.

*

Unwanted **visitor**
depression
called today.

Pretended I was out.

His black dog loiters.

*

Love's virus
took hold.
His moves, once **deft**,
eluded him.
She left.

Bereft.

     *

Their cosy **campfire**
had flames fanned.
Infidelity
fanned flames,
bonfire
Inferno
inextinguishable.

Ashes.

     *

Yattering **haggle**
of the Souk,
debatable tactics;
I bought into your baggage.

Swindled.

*

Your betrayal;
That **stab** of pain
time cannot heal.

Rejection's
dull
ache
lingers.

*

Graceful gazelle
swept across savannah,
Feinted to elude
lion's savage manner.

Scratched roar.

*

He'd **propel** -
she'd repel.
He'd thrust -
she'd trust.

She'd yield -
he reeled.

Commitment.

(4)MEGWAF

wind against **window pane**
  w a i l i n g
not waning
as the light begins to fade

                    *

clumsily
she fell

tripping

slowly
  s
    p
i
  l
    l
i
  n
g
words

/ deftly
not being one of them /

*

tied to kite strings
thoughts fight
    thermal **entanglements**
as we read between lines

*

part of my all
now apart from me

my heart
in **particles**
  .   s
   c a
t
       t
 e   r
        e
       d

*

time screams
like a steam locomotive
whistling **along**
on tracks made of bones

*

definitely not
a deluge
of inspiration

vague **sprinkles**
  no puddles

cloudy
mostly dry

*

a stealthy silence grows
as distance
breathes
out

feeling
  the edges
becoming gaps

*

I've chewed upon this word
too long
  / **shred** its meaning
      lost its flavour

ⒶSHIFTING_VOID

Carved flesh
Crumble bones
She is waxen
She can do nothing
But **wane**

*

Shred my skin
Break me down
Brand my heart
Yet, still,
I remain

*

This **quondam** heartbreak lasts
Aching drifting agony
The past repeats into the present

*

Knocked aside
Torn asunder
Trajectory **askew**
Spiraled out
The path fades
Confused again

     *

Take this splinter fragment
battered crushed thing
immerse it
In your healing waters

     *

solitary figure
Cloaked in loneliness
seafarer's eyes misty
She takes to the oars

     *

I'm in the **market**
For a new soul
Could I steal yours?
Momentarily

*

Grief washes over
Rasping breaths
Gritted teeth
Sprinkle some solace
On my grave

*

Infectious poison
Slow **circulation**
Creeping silently
Through my veins
Carefully now...
She's venomous

*

It shatters
Total detonation
Anatomical desolation
particles atrophy
Blown across
The strangest cosmos

@IMPAUL23

Work dragging
Enthusiasm **waned**
Thinking about you
Pulled me through
Made me smile

*

Don't **haggle** over love
Embrace it at all costs
Let it consume you

*

The day you left
My heart **shred**
Into pieces
Unable
To be healed

*

Watching your lips **glisten**
In the afternoon sun
I long to kiss you

*

You are the **visitor**
That entered my heart
And there you will stay

*

Windows steamed with **condensation**
The heat between us
So intensely hot
So passionate

*

Your words, your beauty, they **propel** my heart through my chest, towards you

*

No **TURBULENCE** is too great for our beautiful, passionate love story to overcome

*

A **seafarer**
Across endless seas
Your heart, love
I come home to thee

*

A **stab** in my heart
Your betrayal
Hurt me
Leaving me broken
Alone

*

Your **cranberry** coloured lipstick tastes so good
when I'm kissing your beautiful lips

*

Knowing you
Seeing you
Wanting you
Provides a **whirlwind** of emotions in me

ⓐCross_Hali

A grieving
heart
dwells in the
Chasm of **exile**
Longing
To be
Reconciled

        *

Combating the **muzzle**
Of sorrow
The poet lets her heart
B
  L   D
    E E in ink

        *

Teardrop's tempo
Plays Diminuendo
Along a **vertebrae**
Of forgotten morrows
Songs of sorrow

*

Nature's
Rhapsody sang
In the wind
Fluttering the petals
Of her flower garden

*

Topple EVERYthing
See it the
other way 🅐🅡🅞🅤🅝🅓
T
  I
    P
      S
        Y, TOPSY,
t
  urvy

uʍop əpısdn

*

She learned to bloom
In the night
Lovely **moonflower**
Aglow in the fight

*

Steaks of rain
Ghostly apparitions
Of **virga**
Bedevil softly
Above sorrows
Haunted cry

*

Galileo's
Heliocentrism
None geocentrism

Investigated
By the inquisition
The accurate heretic

Right too early

@EJ_REINE

Although, we spoke in different phonetics
We knew our hearts were completely **magnetic**

*

her **wingspan** had been diminished
and when they fell off she was finished

*

a **satellite**
on a
starry night
did not diminish
the moon's dancing delight

*

Truth Proof
Reflections Soothe
I am one
I am both
Horns and Halo

*

dissolved like
water droplets
shattered hearts
fall apart
often
for hate
or sport

*

Weaponize your anger
Make yourself better
When you morph
You won't be lost

*

Come on
Let's face it babe
I am so dearly
Completely clearly
Irreplaceable

*

the distraction **machinations**
fed the masses
who were dedicated
to the orange baby

    *

His laughter merely **propelled** our ever after
His smile confused my weary mind

    *

My words can only be **Effective**
If they are clearly perceived as Affective

    *

incinerate the memories
they shall burn with eternity
rather than live in me

    *

in an **opium** haze
reality loses my gaze
fantasy becomes a maze

@ProsSpeaks

I
Will
Not
Swoon

For
I
Have
Learnt

That
Lif/(*ov*)/e

Isn't
That
Simple

*

Let's
Have
A
stab
At
happiness.

What
Have
We
Got
To
Lose?

*

My
poem-s
Feel
Quite
imponderous

The
#fatal
Effect

Of
Saturation
Amidst
Abundant
Brilliance

(A)STULL_MITCHELL

All those thoughts
Words I couldn't say
Remain in **boxes**
On shelves today

*

Stoking the **campfire**
Embers crackle, flames flicker
Beauty to admire
Warmth surrounds her

*

Opportunistic **Imposter**
Unfortunately not so true
Left me feeling hurtful
Lost, sad, blue

*

Sailing through their duties
Swabbing decks gleam
Enchanted island beauties
A **seafarer**'s dream

*

Sinful expressions
Sprinkles of magical dust
Intimate sessions
Spellbound in love or lust

*

Days into weeks
Weeks into years
Years **becoming** a lifetime
Spent missing you

*

Aviary of confinement
Guilt in their words
Songs of discontent
Sung by **jailbirds**

*

Thoughts on a page
Ransom held apart
Emotional **hostage**
Affairs of the heart

*

Although you may continue your search, just know, my feelings will never **wane**.

*

To **retrieve** personal effects
A duty role
My heart it affects
Heavy toll

*

I need honesty, to **preserve** the last bit of dignity I have left.

*

One of my dreams
My **lofty** expectation
By any means
Cause for celebration

@CHAMOMILESPELLS

Dreams imagine
being real

reality wishes
to be unreal

dual wheels
spinning surreal

        *

Nature's beauty
mesmerizing **trapdoor**

ceaselessly galore
to explore

alluring charm
leaves craving more

        *

Trust becomes
a **cautious** hope
walking on tightrope
for a heart that broke

*

Thought you
would **entertain**

but you entered
life

to taint it
with pain

*

Words can
shatter

fragile heart
matter

broken pieces
can't be glued
that **scatter**

*

Recklessly thrown
penniless laughter
becomes priceless

when bound to chase it
hopelessly endless

*

Locked gazes of yesterday
tethering hearts of today
unlocking **entanglements**
of every tomorrow

*

Eyes shooting
mesmerizing arrows
pierce my heart **askew**

Igniting passionate fire
without rescue

@WittyNameSoon

Her breath
lost
in **fog** clouds
Misty words running
ahead
of his heart

*

Looking at the
sky
the brightest
star,
inviting you to come **visit**
Me

(A)Tap3dUpHeart

I lay to the ground
under **pacify** sky
soothing
mind adrift
a cloud.

*

Panache of
wind strumming
the star strings
acoustical sky beats
thunder wave serenade.

*

With breathing musical notes
I **punch** little light holes
to beat of heart.

*

veins **galvanize** in love
to flesh skies heated
heart a melting of beat .

*

bottled **seafarer** heart
sunken breath to
shackled beat
descend
from shore
to abyssal.

*

Eyes **shred** through
reading
countless words

inked tears
drenched upon
naked paper coat.

*

We **absorb** to the rain
like jam on a warm scone
windy wintersday.

*

Feverish sky
rivers flood
over fallen trees
thunder needle prick
split soil trembling.

*

I do not count **anymore**
the hours
become weeks
without you in them.

*

within wings of paper folded planes
his poetry lays , **broadening**
onto heart's runway.

*

From **afar** stars
blanket my eyes
to dream within moon pillow
tears sleep.

@RAJIV‖INDIA

While **haggling**
You struggle
dealing hearts
Where giving
Is gaining
Losing is
Winning

*

Lofty writing
Is cultivated skill
Praise worthy always
Beautiful expressions
Get ornamental
Glitter.

*

murmurs as heard
Bombard inside
Besides rhythm
Who understand
Silent noise
Unheard cry.

*

Seafarers meet
Mermaids
But they have to keep
Promise
So they return back.

*

Scattered stars
Can not light path
Guides direction
To move in the dark.

*

Always when tide
Ocean's waves climb high
To kiss moon which is **afar**

*

In that **ransack**
There's an urge
A vigour
To find oneself
Into others

*

Her simplicity
Earned a **panache**
The elegance of
Peahen walking
On jungle trail

*

What you expect
From grandmother's
boxes
Her precious
Memories
Associated with
Each articles

*

imprint still
Found on the
Heart
Long after
The departure
Of the **visitors**

@SonuPrajai08

His thoughts,
Her favourite music,
His scent,
Her reverie;
All playing
On **loop**

*

"Gratified" his second name
He derived contentment
From the **plethora** of her thoughts

*

One look at him
I am ecstatic
Our gaze locked
We are **restless**

ⒶWVINEET1

The **soliloquy** rendered
From the cliff edge
Echoes the symphony of true love

*

Pawns bravely resist
The **surreptitious** approach to castle the king
Queen smiles wickedly

*

It was an **optical** trap
The grandmother's cloak
Behind it hid a wolf

*

When love began to cool
Condensation made relations opaque
Frosty talks became normal

*

The excessive **effuse**
In the presentation was to hide
Hollowness of the content

*

Ever wonder
From where
Mother
Would **replenish**
Her love
For us
Uncaring children

*

I **rifle** through memories
For that one moment
I promised to cherish forever

*

A full moon
Over an empty meadow
A **hiraeth** induced madness
Overwhelms me

*

All got a **slice** of luck
Mine was smaller
Yet with most pluck

*

The tin **boxes**
Lay forgotten
Stuffed with happiness
Of simple lives
From yesteryears

*

The **lissome** maid was made to wait
Prince was checking the horse's gait

ⒶAflameTarot

The Mynah bird
is
the veranda's
white spider's
visitor
and eater
early
Morning

                  *

a curious fellow
in need
at the place
speaking through
stuttering **rouge** lips

                  *

Your **being**
is like
the fresh crispness
of
newly sun kissed
washed sheets

*

near, #afar
past, future
decision, aspiration
ancestors, seed
house, country
near, **afar**
Present

*

Grounding aroma
of Cedarwood oil
soothes
a **texture**
of uneasy
sharp
heart beats

*

A vapid
mind's **trapdoor**
is to soar
amongst
the colourful spores
of pictoralization

*

sucking on a milk bottle, tails wagging back and forth, one **jocund** lamby

*

innocence
l
  a
   n
    d
     l
      o
       c
        k
         e
          d
in
a **whirlwind** of dreams
and
possibilities
a recipe
For
adventures

(4)IDEANUMBER13

Topple ideologies
Statues fall
Topple dictators
Freedom call
Topple fears
Dreams stand tall!

*

Tired. Hungry. Alone.

nevertheless

Determined. Steadfast. Resolute.

nevertheless

Success will be reached.

Finally!

*

Success Forgotten
WIns ignored
Countless hours
Hardwork
Matters no more

Redundancy really sucks!

*

I know my stuff
Yet **being** interviewed
is really tough

Vacancy?

HIRE ME!

@SMITCHELWRITES

Those unspoken glances
lost between a **fog** of
smoke clouding their
lascivious thoughts...

*

Your words taste
like holy sin making
my mind drip with
salacious thoughts...

*

Your words **entertain**
those salacious ideas
roaming from my mind
to your thoughts.

*

So many **restless**
nights with unspoken
truths left between
the moon and stars.

*

His lips, **unraveling**
her thoughts as he
penetrates her mind
with sinful pleasures.

*

Be **cautious** of words
that lead to illusions
of the mind and heart…

*

Your words **replenish**
my mind, body, and
soul when I hear
your voice.

@FREE_THINKERIST

Expose says

There's way
Too many
Unutterable
Judgemental
Cunts
In this world today

*

Absorb thoughts
Receive new ideas
Ruminate
Deliberate

Never negate
Your impeccable
Intellectual
Autonomy

*

Gordon
Was hoarding
Lots
Of chocolate
Sneaking
Eating

His ass's
Mass
Massively
Broadened

*

Prioritise
Honesty
Over lies
Freedom
Over dumb
Rationalism
Over
Nationalism
Tolerance
Over
Abhorrence

*

Jocund Joe
Was a merry bloke
Couldn't handle the drink
Though

Boked
Fucking tornadoes

*

I estimate
I detest
Innumerable 'mates'

Whoever
grates
my nerves

I now
swerve

*

Whirlwinds of creativity
Unfurled sins, from minds so free

More prompts
Promptly, please!

(A) JEAN ROE MARTIN

Measure
Your treasure
In moments
Of laughter
A **penniless**
Wealth
Greatly
Sought after.

*

An atmospheric,
Shimmering,
Luminescent
Waterfall
Flickers
Into sight...
Northern Lights
Galvanize
Magical delight.

*

One star...
Time traveling
From **afar**,
Illuminated
Christmas night
With a miraculous light.

*

Pain
Always
An uninvited
Visitor.
You invade
My body,
I become
Your
Prisoner.

*

Do not
Scatter
Your
Energy
But burn
Slowly
Like
Beeswax
Long lasting,
Steadfast.

*

Pages of
Imaginative
Print
Do more than
Entertain me...
Books
Absolutely
Sustain me.

@Vlad_Lioncourt

She was a **collage**,
of all things
beautiful and sultry.
And loved him.

*

Winter's day,
Shining in low wattage
Its somber mood
Doth hold me **hostage**.

*

Giants of beauty
Propel me towards
A joyful reunion
With peace and tranquility.

ⓐYONAR

Caffeine, liquid **vertebrae**,
Keep me straight —
Blessed insomnia,
Hold my nightmares at bay.

*

Saturated with choice,
We find ourselves with
A **plethora** of all
But freedom.

*

With the dimming light
Behind the **windowpane**,
So faded the pain
Of being.

*

Sifting through ashes,
Hoping to **preserve**
Fragments of who you were
To me.

*

Aggravated thoughts —
Ejaculated, **catapulted**,
Burying whoever listens
Under unrelenting
Verbal avalanches
Of discontent.

*

This broken **husk**
Where love once teemed,
Now devoid
Of all but memories.

*

Fear, hate, uncertainty --
We stand upon the watershed,
Witnessing the **genesis**...
Of what?

*

Loneliness the norm --
Consideration **bookended**
By social expectation.
Generations suffering
Legacies of conformity.

*

Charity is fashion
In this two-tier society —
Shreds of humanity,
Stripped of compassion.

@SpiritDDrmWeavr

Channel your creativity: imagine all you can be, **orchestrate** your reality, determine destiny.

ⒶPONDERODA

We count down
Before we drown
The noise of protest.

For the best

***countless**

@DaniGraceWrites

You **circulate**
Through my veins
Breathe life
Into these lungs
One heartbeat
Synchronicity.

*

I **rifle** through
Inner files of mind
Remembering the time
Innocence was mine.

*

Night falls on deep seas
With **glistening** melodies
Stars sing in glad hearts.

*

Brilliance
Through pure
Art of the **shred**,
Van Halen's axe
Rocks Heaven's bed.

for Eddie Van Halen

*

I'd rather a dagger
Stabbed into my heart,
Than see your back again.

*

Through spattered
Windowpanes,
Minds and bodies
Ripped in twain;
Raging monsters
Roar again.

*

Spouted **soliloquies**
Bounce off drums
Piercing hearts
Purloined by the
Shadows of sorrow.

*

Our lips
Are **magnets**
Which connect
Never reversing
Desired effects
Of perfect polarity.

*

Catapulted
Beyond stars
Spun through
Riveting liaisons
Discovering terrible
Fantastical things
Inside imagination.

(A) FIZZY TWIZLER

Murmuring caresses

       I think I'm in heaven

Don't stop pulling my long tresses

       *

Big Bad Bear,
Hiding in the **woods**...
Stole my honey!
SOS sent, Winnie.

       *

Countless they are,

Skin cells all over me,

Each one, breathes your name.

       *

Tiny **particles** explode
Prism of colours appear
Butterflies in tummies
Sing
First kiss

*

Your invisible **deft** fingers
Pluck gently
My heart strings

Tuning finely
Synchronized heartbeats

*

New Moon bright
Unfurling my **Vertebrae**
Loadsa hair
I become WereFizzy
Ha beware!

*

Nook
Of his neck
I took a bite
Oh a tasty jugular 'twas

*

Thievery of my mind
When you stole my heart
    With words of poetry

*

In your embrace
I feel your **reverence**
Beating from your heart's
Soothing vibrations

*

I **sift** desperately

Through pieces
Of my broken heart
Nevertheless

I'm too late

@STARFISH_72

Reverence
my father's gentle nature
my mother's selflessness
sharing the sky as one

*

Sprinkle your presence
where this day begins & ends
gratitude will pour over

*

Countless times
I have found solace
in the kindness
& hope we share

*

Immersed in change
I wish I could still love you
the earthly way

*

A **collage**
of natural blessings
continuously flowing
ever returning to
a grateful heart

*

The world spins
inside my head
a **foggy** morning
the window
stays unlocked

*

Genesis of loneliness
to feel disconnected from
the one you want the most

*

Illusions exposed
you will not follow
you will not play
the fool **anymore**

*

Second youth **coalescing**
an erinaceous haircut
the newbie at bingo
will stand out

*

Take me **away**
so I can think again
let nature feel my interest

*

I'm searching
the reality of lost socks
circulating in my drawers
absorbing patience

*

An early October afternoon
in our part of the world
autumn is **circulating**

ⒶJuliusOrlovsky

The sun haggled
With rain clouds
Until they collaborated
And created a rainbow

*

Living in shadows
 and ashes
searching for
meteor showers
to illuminate
the dark.

*

Countless ways
 to find light

      yet
    she was still
      lost
    in the dark.

*

Absorbing the pale
    moonlight
      into my soul
        to become one
          with the night

*

I was overly exuberant,

positively **rambunctious**

and boisterous.

Manifesting mischief and

mayhem aplenty.

*

broadening her horizons by leaping over stars and swimming in the milky way.

*

She often **ransacks**
her brain to discover
when it all began to
   u
      n
         r
            a
               v
                  e
                    l

*

Always watching from **afar**

Too afraid to approach
Too afraid to look away

ⓐPOETRYIN13

pointless
unravelling
over the
imaginary

there is a
forest dying
from inhumane
Debauchery

*

there is a forest
haunted by
its expansive
murmuring,
from soil to
overstory

*

stars are
suspended above
cotton ball cloud
coverage while
night bleeds,
overturning
daylight

*

people fall to
pieces, stay
silent in
boxes

send themselves
someplace,
hopefully
better

*

never
being first
to burst
into novas
does not
make us
scandalous
imposters

*

there is
a forest
where trees
never **fret**

the silent
sun always
rises

Epilogue

Fear

Long Live #vss365

There's not much about which I'm cautious in life; however, I did wait until turning thirty-three before getting my first tattoo. See that it was going to be inked into my skin for life, the design had to be in relation to something about which I wouldn't wake up one day after my eightieth birthday and damn the shriveled Tweety bird all to hell. So, instead I got what I refer to as my Big Gay Jew tattoo: a rainbow Star of David.

So it went for the next three tattoos I had artists etch onto my body over the next fourteen years. But there was no question as to what would become the fifth: a flaming-red #vss365 on my right forearm, which I had done several months ago.

Like the rest, it has marked my body permanently. I had always wanted to be a writer, and strangely enough, a waiter in the restaurant industry - a fine profession I'd held for twenty-six years; not a minute of which I would consider replacing.

I wrote my first book at thirteen. Over the years that followed, I created poetry and short stories, none of which was saved. Upon turning twenty-six, I decided to write a memoir. After a few false starts, I sat down at the age of forty-one and wrote the first two hundred pages of memories before scrapping them.

They weren't right.

It wasn't until some significant things happened to me upon turning forty-four that the timing had felt right, so I took six months of that year to write and complete my first book, a memoir called *What's Become Of Me*. Despite being poorly edited, I submitted the final product for review and received several positive notices in local Milwaukee publications.

With the publication, I premiered my *very* independent publishing imprint, Steering 23 Publications. Over the course of four years, I went on to write more than twenty books in my book name plus two *nom de plumes*: a second memoir, a YA novel, a stand-alone novel, two poetry collections, two mystery novels (meant to be the start of a series), a serial erotica novel, two nightstand classics (smut), and nine short story collections.

Although *What's Become Of Me* sold 150 copies (a respectable amount for someone who literally does all the work on their own), sales for subsequent works were dismal; some titles not even selling a single copy. People enjoyed the writing. Merely calling my editorialization skills "lacking" would be like saying the movie *Mars Needs Moms* was a financial success.

So I took a break and stumbled into Twitter's Writing Community. It wasn't until I found #vss365, a daily prompt word exercise for writers to create stories and poetry using 280 characters, minus the eight needed for the hashtag plus one space separating it from the author's work. I found it exhilarating, and was mesmerized by the incredible things that unfolded on my computer screen from other scribes. It changed the way I wrote and helped me with editing.

In all honesty, #vss365 changed my life. I am a fierce ally of the prompt, its participants, hosts, and marvelous people who bring it to fruition. It is the healthiest obsession I've ever had.

That's no exaggeration.

Without #vss365, I would still be struggling and releasing books no one would read. Not only that, I knew they were incomplete. Someday in the near future I plan to go back and edit all of my work and put out products I can truly be proud of.

So, I felt it necessary to show my gratitude. I gave @Making_Fiction and his ambassadors (@derickijohnson, @alva1206, @voimaoy, @_irene_dreams_, @patchiesteve) along with some prompt past prompt hosts (@EdHaiku575, @AvyeAndonellis, @ESWarriorPoet, @fhaedra, @RozLevens) and hosts of other prompts (@jason_h_abbott ((@SciFanSat and #2wordprompt)), @somaxdatta ((@52WeekPoetry)), @FrankieInParis ((@JuxThis)), @ConverStory, @craytusjones ((#SatSplat)), @whistberry ((@WhistprPrompts)), @AmandaJK_ ((@vssmurder)), @WhimsyCheshire ((#36FF)), @juliusorofsky ((#5wordspoet and #7wordspoet)), @MadQueenStorm ((#MadVerse and #SlamWords)), @TransGurlWriter ((@TransWords)), @atreya2112 ((@atreyasverse)) and @i_poet ((#123Words and #becomingfragile)).

*

It's a high honor to include the words of these outstanding creatives about whose friendship I must pinch myself on a daily basis.

Thank you for writing.

Thank you for keeping my vital signs up and running.

Thank you for putting up with me.

Thank you for being such great sports.
Thank you for being around.
Thank you for being the definition of everything.

Scott Christopher Beebe
12/24/20
4:23pm
Milwaukee, WI

FEAR

Forensic love is
Everywhere
Arms entwined; minds combined
Racing hearts, our love starts

@Making_Fiction

*

beyond the land of **fear**,
wide sea beckons to
the blue horizon

@VoimaOy

*

Hiding in my closet
Golem of my **fear**
Ravenously hungry
And imminently near

@DerickiJohnson

＊

Fear has you
in a death grip
don't get choked out
~fight back

@_Irene_Dreams_

＊

Turning **fear**

Into learning

Is the most important lesson

I taught myself today

@Alvai206

＊

Shrinks,
If unfed
Leaves, but never goes far
Before rushing back
My **fear**

@PatchieSteve

❋

Breathe,
Let the dread subside.
I'll quieten your **fear** -
Caress your pounding heart.

@RozLevens

❋

Known are Old Answers.
For the new,
Shred your **fear**
Of the unknown.

@ESWarriorPoet

❋

Silver Lining

I **fear** less lately,
I love more greatly
Than I ever did before.

@AvyeAndonellis

❋

Fear of missing out
Don't!
Can't have it all
In 13 words
Or less

@EdHaikus75

*

What time
is future

How long
this train

After **fear**
loses the game

@Fhaedra

*

Fear
A four-letter word
That has prevented
The birth of heroes
And authors

@J<small>ASON</small>_H_A<small>BBOTT</small>

*

Words have
deserted you,
I **fear**

So many thoughts
imprisoned behind
pleading eyes

@W<small>HISTBERRY</small>

*

"Stop following me"

"I am getting closer"

"You shadows suck"

"Live in **fear**"

@C<small>ONVER</small>S<small>TORY</small>

✱

My greatest **fear**
stares back at me
from the reflection
in the mirror
    @SOMAXDATTA

✱

A human existence stricken
by **fear** of a bug unleashed
through social media.

    @I_POET

✱

Fairytale **fear**;
stygian black
opaque nightmares
stunned by the
eroding nostalgia
of you.

    @ITSAMBERJAYDE

✱

Fear might linger in
The darkness, but
Only you can
Keep it alive

    @TransGurlWriter

     ✸

she felt no fear
the angel of death
spoke the language of crows

    @MadQueenStorm

     ✸

Lost & alone
Darkness creeps closer
A **fear** overwhelming
Engulfing & suffocating
Me

    @AmandaJK_

     ✸

My greatest **fear**
Is that you will discover
The real me
And run

@FrankieInParis

*

Complexity never falters
 To fall
   On the living..
Folding chaos
   To **fear**..
     Unkempt..

@Atreya2112

*

Face your fears
feel the festering,
the wounds beneath.
Disconnect your disease,
Survive.

@WhimsyCheshire

*

Writing poems
to flush out the
 emotions I fear
to say out loud.

@JuliusOrlovsky

*

In darkness,
I wade through knee-deep water.
Fear is nothing but fuel.

@CraytusJones

*

never let fear
take hold -
removing
its clutches is
an entire
horror story

@PoetryIni3

Scott Christopher Beebe

is the author of nearly 30 books, most of which are poetry and short story collections as well as several novels. He has been the editor of seven anthologies including pieces of flash fiction, poetry and short stories written by people from Twitter's vast Writing Community which spans the globe. The first of these efforts, *Crispy Rooftop Conversation Stories*, was released in November, 2019. After the completion of *Poetry In 13, Volume Three*, Scott plans to release two more anthologies in short order: one erotica (*Quintessential Universal Erotica*), the other's theme is horror (*Abominations Told By Zombies*).

Mr. Beebe lives in Milwaukee with two cats and an addiction to #vss365 for which he doesn't seek treatment or a cure.

M.

Printed in Great Britain
by Amazon